THE
RENAISSANCE

Medal showing Bramante's design for the new St. Peter's

Fragment from a world map of 1537

Model of Leonardo's flying machine

The Wilton Diptych, c.1395

Fra Angelico, *The Deposition*, c.1440–45

Laocoön, 2nd–1st century B.C.

Leonardo da Vinci's drawing of *Vitruvian Man*, c.1487

Ghiberti's self-portrait, from the Baptistery doors, 1425–52

EYEWITNESS ART
THE RENAISSANCE

ALISON COLE

Joachim Patenier,
*St. Jerome in a
Rocky Landscape,*
1515

Titian, *The Assumption
and Coronation of
the Virgin,*
1516–18

Ghiberti, *Joseph in
Egypt,* from the
Baptistery doors,
1425–52

Masaccio, *The Expulsion,* c.1427

DORLING KINDERSLEY
LONDON • NEW YORK • STUTTGART
IN ASSOCIATION WITH
THE NATIONAL GALLERY, LONDON

Michelangelo,
Moses, c.1515

Raphael, *Portrait of Baldassare Castiglione*, c.1514–15

Woodblock of Albrecht Dürer's
St. Jerome in His Study, 1492

A DORLING KINDERSLEY BOOK

Editor Luisa Caruso
Art editor Tracy Hambleton-Miles
Assistant editor Peter Jones
Assistant designer Simon Murrell
Senior editor Gwen Edmonds
Managing editor Sean Moore
Managing art editor Toni Kay
Picture researchers Julia Harris-Voss,
Jo Evans
DTP designer Zirrinia Austin
Production controller Meryl Silbert

This Eyewitness ®/™ Art book
first published in Great Britain in 1994 by
Dorling Kindersley Limited,
9 Henrietta Street, London WC2E 8PS

A CIP catalogue record for this book is
available from the British Library

ISBN 0 7513 104 76

Colour reproduction by GRB Editrice s.r.l.
Printed in Italy by A. Mondadori Editore, Verona

Andrea del Castagno,
The Youthful David, c.1450

Reliquary containing
St. Dominic's skull

Hugo van der Goes, *Portinari Altarpiece*, c.1476–78

Contents

Albrecht Dürer,
St. Anthony in Front of the City, 1519

What is the Renaissance?

THE LABEL "RENAISSANCE" (French: "rebirth") is usually applied to a period in the history of Western Europe stretching from the early 14th century to the mid- to late 16th century. In writings of the time, however, the term was used more specifically to describe a movement – the new spirit of rebirth in art and literature. It first applied to the revived study of classical learning, popularized by the Italian poet and Latin scholar Petrarch (1304–74), who rejected the Middle Ages as a period of "darkness"; later Erasmus of Rotterdam (c.1469–1536) welcomed new translations of ancient texts and a "purer literature". The idea of rebirth in art was developed by the Florentine art historian Giorgio Vasari (1511–74). He claimed, in his *Lives of the Most Excellent Painters, Sculptors, and Architects* (1550), that art had been reborn in Italy in about 1250 and had progressed through "childhood" and "youth" to its 16th-century maturity. It is this self-conscious awareness of being part of something new and superior that gives a confident and cohesive character to the Renaissance period. Now, with the advantage of historical perspective, the Renaissance is seen as building on, rather than breaking with, its medieval heritage, and northern Europe is considered as important as Italy in the development of new ideals and techniques. North and south of the Alps, there was a new interest in naturalism: to the Italians, their ancient Roman past held the key to truth and nature in art; the Flemish found truth in the observation of nature. The interchange between these two approaches is one of the determining factors of Renaissance style.

ENGLAND

London •

Brug
Ghe
Lille
Tourn

Paris •

NAVARRE

ARAGON

CASTILE

THE TAZZA FARNESE
The Renaissance Italians idealized the classical past, seeing their own period as a second "Golden Age". Antique works, like this Alexandrian agate bowl (2nd–1st century B.C.), were prized for their techniques (once lost) and were often copied. Botticelli adapted the mythological figures of the Etesian winds, who ensured the Nile's fertility, for his *Birth of Venus* (below).

THE BIRTH OF VENUS
Sandro Botticelli; c.1486; 175 x 275 cm (70 x 108¼ in); tempera on canvas
This famous mythological picture by Sandro Botticelli (pp. 32–33) illustrates the birth of Venus, goddess of love – and the rebirth of the ancient ideal of beauty in the Early Renaissance. Botticelli, like earlier artists, has borrowed the pose of an antique Roman statue, the *Medici Venus* (p. 19), for his Venus and altered it to contemporary Florentine tastes. He has refined and simplified all the figures, enhancing these effects by depicting long, flowing hair and fluttering draperies. The rhythmic forms of Gothic art – the style of medieval northern Europe (p. 63) – are fused with the styling of ancient Roman reliefs. A similar mingling of medieval and ancient influences appears in much of Early Renaissance art.

Boundary of the Holy Roman Empire

- Amsterdam
- Antwerp
- Brussels · Cologne
- FLANDERS
SAXONY

HOLY ROMAN EMPIRE

BURGUNDY
- Nuremberg
- Basel
- Augsburg
DUCHY OF
MILAN
MANTUA
REPUBLIC OF
VENICE
Verona
Milan · · Venice
SAVOY Padua
Genoa · · Bologna
· Ferrara
DUCHY OF
FERRARA
DUCHY OF
MODENA
· Avignon
Florence
Pisa · · Urbino
· Arezzo
Siena · Perugia
REPUBLIC
OF GENOA
· Rome
PAPAL
STATES
REPUBLIC OF
FLORENCE
DUCHY OF
PIOMBINO
REPUBLIC
OF SIENA
Naples ·
KINGDOM OF
NAPLES

SARDINIA

SICILY

A political map
of c.1450 showing
the main artistic
centres in Italy and
northern Europe

SELF-PORTRAIT
*Albrecht Dürer; 1500; 170 x 124.5 cm
(67 x 49 in); oil on canvas*
One of the driving forces for
change in the Renaissance was the
growing professionalization of the
artist. Artists won recognition as
creative innovators, rather than
skilled craftsmen like carpenters
or tailors. They consolidated their
new social and economic status by
developing greater skills, such as
the mathematical techniques of
perspective (p. 28) and proportion
(p. 30), and composing theoretical
treatises. Painting, sculpture, and
architecture were gradually seen
as part of the liberal arts, and the
idea of the accomplished "universal
man" developed. The greatest
figure of the Northern Renaissance,
the German artist Albrecht Dürer
(pp. 40–41), was very conscious of
his own artistic status. He painted
this solemn self-portrait "in the
manner of Christ" to acknowledge
his "God-given" creative powers.
However, the transformation of
the artist's status occurred earlier
in Italy than in northern Europe.
When Dürer visited Italy in 1505–6,
he wrote back to his Nuremberg
correspondent: "here I am a gentleman, at home I am a parasite."

CHRIST AS RULER OF THE UNIVERSE
Dürer's *Self-portrait* has the majesty
of this Byzantine mosaic of Christ
(c.1190) in Monreale Cathedral,
Sicily. In the Middle Ages,
Italy was dominated by
the art of the Greek
Byzantine Empire, but
Renaissance Italians
thought it "crude", in
contrast to naturalistic
ancient Roman art.

*The Virgin's
idealized beauty
suggests her
spiritual purity*

Renaissance centres

The Renaissance covers such a vast
sweep of time, and embraces so broad a
geographical area, that it is now divided
into manageable periods. The "Early
Renaissance" usually refers to Italian
art in Tuscany in about 1400 to 1500,
centring on the city-state of Florence
and the work of artists like Giotto,
Masaccio, Donatello, and Botticelli.
The "High Renaissance" relates
to art in Papal Rome, Florence,
and Venice, from about
1500 to 1540/80, focusing
on Michelangelo, Raphael,
Leonardo (who bridges the
Early and High Renaissance),
and Titian. The "Northern
Renaissance" encompasses
the art of the countries
in northern Europe (the
"North"), about 1400 to
1550, including artists as
diverse as Dürer from
Nuremberg and Van
Eyck from Bruges.

PIETA
*Michelangelo; c.1498–1500;
height: 1.74 m (5 ft 9 in); marble*
This monumental sculpture was
made by the High Renaissance
master Michelangelo (pp. 54–55)
for a French cardinal, who specified
that it should be "the most beautiful
work in marble that exists today in
Rome". A *pietà* (Italian: "pity") is
a Northern medieval subject in
which the Virgin Mary mourns
her dead son. Michelangelo's
sculpture is the first Italian
version of the theme. It
shows the dead Christ
lying across the Virgin's
lap, and reflects a
Renaissance tendency,
inspired by the work of
the Greek philosopher
Plato, to idealize the
human form.

7

The impact of Giotto

THE FLORENTINE GIOTTO DI BONDONE (c.1267–1337) was celebrated in his lifetime for the revolutionary naturalism of his new style. What so impressed Giotto's contemporaries was the emotional intensity and dramatic realism of his art. The famous poet Dante (p. 12) heralded him as the foremost among painters, while the writer Boccaccio praised him for bringing the art of painting "back to light" after centuries of darkness. Giotto was credited with translating what was held to be the "rude manner" of the Byzantine era (p. 7) into the natural style that was then associated with ancient Roman art. This is clearly displayed in the best-preserved of his works, the great cycle of wall paintings in the Arena Chapel, Padua, which was executed in the popular medium of fresco (p. 63). Giotto's use of monumental human forms to tell stories simply and dramatically set an example for artists from Masaccio (pp. 18–19) to Michelangelo (pp. 54–55).

MEDIEVAL CONVENTIONS
This stained-glass window from Cologne Cathedral (1280) is an example of early storytelling in art. It shows the Annunciation, when the Angel Gabriel tells the Virgin that she will "conceive and bear a son". The Annunciation was first portrayed in Gothic church art, using easily recognizable gestures, symbols – such as the dove of the Holy Spirit – and inscriptions.

THE GOLDEN LEGEND
Many images from the lives of the Virgin and saints were based on stories from *The Golden Legend* (left), written by Jacobus da Voragine in the 13th century.

THE ARENA CHAPEL
The Arena Chapel was built for the wealthy Italian merchant Enrico Scrovegni in his home city of Padua. It was dedicated to the Annunciation, and soon after its completion, the young Giotto was commissioned to decorate it (c.1305) with scenes from the lives of the Virgin and Christ. The vividly coloured stories, surrounded by painted frames, are arranged in three tiers above pairs of virtues and vices, which are painted to look like statues (far right).

The Meeting at the Golden Gate

GIOTTO DI BONDONE *c.1306;*
200 x 185 cm (78¾ x 72¾ in); fresco
In this moving scene from the Arena Chapel, Giotto shows the meeting of Joachim and Anna (the future parents of the Virgin) before the Golden Gate of Jerusalem – a story related in *The Golden Legend*. Joachim has had a revelation while in the wilderness; his wife, Anna, has also been visited by an angel and told that she will bear a child. Returning to tell Anna, Joachim is met by his wife, and their kiss – set dramatically in the front plane of the picture – symbolizes the moment of the Virgin's Immaculate Conception.

Detail of Joachim and Anna, from *The Meeting at the Golden Gate* (below left)

Detail of Christ and Judas, from *The Betrayal of Christ* (below)

MOTIONS OF THE MIND
Giotto's use of facial expression and gesture gives his figures immense psychological power. The tenderness of Joachim and Anna's embrace (far left) is expressed by their overlapping forms and gently encircling hands. Both lean forward and their eyes meet in an intense gaze of shared joy and suffering. In the *Betrayal* (left; below), Judas's taut arm is disguised by drapery. His lips are pursed, his eyes shrouded by his forehead – the antithesis of Christ, who meets his treachery with a calm, steady gaze. The soldiers, pressed between their profiles, add to the dramatic tension.

CHRISTIAN MORALITY
This toppling figure symbolizes the vice of Inconstancy and is one of the series of virtues and vices along the lower wall. Such figures were popular in medieval painting and sculpture, and were used by the church to give shape to abstract moral ideas. The scene of the Last Judgement often accompanies them as a moral warning (Giotto painted one on the entrance wall).

GIOTTO'S NARRATIVE MASTERPIECE
Giotto's mosaic of the *Navicella* (Italian: "Little Ship"), which decorated the old St. Peter's Basilica in Rome (p. 51), was praised for the diversity of its poses: each expresses "a disturbed mind". It was later damaged, and is now best shown in engravings (left).

The Betrayal of Christ
GIOTTO DI BONDONE *c.1306;*
200 x 185 cm (78¾ x 72¾ in); fresco
This scene from the *Life of Christ* in the Arena Chapel illustrates the moment when Christ is betrayed to his enemies by his disciple, Judas. As Christ stands among soldiers, Judas encircles him with his cloak and identifies him with a kiss of greeting. As was customary, Giotto has included another episode within the scene – that of St. Peter cutting off the ear of the High Priest's servant. The High Priest is shown directing the gaze of the viewer with his pointing finger.

Painting in Siena

THE ART OF THE ITALIAN CITY-STATE of Siena developed its own particular style in the 14th century. It was dominated by Duccio di Buoninsegna (active 1278–1319), who had as great an impact on Sienese and French painting as his contemporary Giotto had on Florentine art. Duccio looked to Italy's Byzantine tradition (p. 7), combining its bold linear style, splendid colouring, and surface patterns with a new human intimacy. His followers and pupils, among them Ambrogio Lorenzetti (active 1319–48) and Simone Martini (active 1315–44), built on his stylish innovations. Lorenzetti created naturalistic images filled with anecdotal detail, while Martini, serving at the papal court in Avignon, produced works of great ornament and opulence. Later, such minute observation and decorative elegance gave rise to an alternative Renaissance style, known as "International Gothic" (pp. 16–17).

SIENA CATHEDRAL
Between 1250 and 1350, Siena's Cathedral was radically enlarged: the improvements included a new dome, a spectacular new facade by Giovanni Pisano (p. 19), the bell tower, and a refurbished interior. After Siena's unexpected victory in battle over Florence in 1260, the Cathedral became the focus of ritual celebration and thanksgiving.

A reconstruction of Duccio's *Maestà*

The Annunciation
(right)

THE ANNUNCIATION
Duccio di Buoninsegna; 1308–11;
43.2 x 43.8 cm (17 x 17¼ in); tempera on panel
This small panel is part of a vast double-sided altarpiece, made by Duccio and his workshop for Siena Cathedral, known as the *Maestà* (an image of the Virgin "in majesty"). In June 1311, the altarpiece was carried in joyful procession from Duccio's workshop to the Cathedral, astounding the crowds with its size and splendour. In 1771, the altarpiece was dismantled and several of its panels were sold abroad. This reconstruction (left) shows its front. The Virgin and Child are enthroned in majesty in the centre, and scenes from the life of the Virgin (including episodes from Christ's childhood) appear above and below: *The Annunciation* begins the narrative cycle on the *"predella"* (plinth; p. 63). The back was painted in similar fashion, with more than 30 scenes from the life of Christ.

ALLEGORY OF GOOD GOVERNMENT
Ambrogio Lorenzetti; 1338;
2.40 x 14 m (7 ft 10 in x 46 ft); fresco
Siena's great town hall – the Palazzo Pubblico – shared centre-stage with the Cathedral. Its rooms were decorated with murals ranging from successful military campaigns and disgraced rebels, to *maestàs*. For the Peace Room, Lorenzetti painted his famous *Allegory of Good and Bad Government. The Effect of Good Government in the City and Its Countryside* (right) faithfully illustrates city statutes (for example, no coats of arms were to decorate the outsides of buildings), while the figure of Security, holding a criminal on the gallows, floats in the sky. Lorenzetti presents a vision of a well-governed city and countryside, where the nobility, merchants, and labourers go about their tasks. It is also an astonishingly naturalistic picture of Siena, the Arbia Valley, and the main road to Rome.

THE ANNUNCIATION

Simone Martini and Lippo Memmi; 1333; 265 x 305 cm (104¼ x 120 in); tempera on panel

In 1333, Simone Martini painted his own altarpiece for Siena Cathedral, assisted by his brother-in-law, Lippo Memmi. It depicts the Annunciation: this was the first time that the subject had been chosen to be the main image of an altarpiece. The Angel Gabriel's words to the Virgin, "Hail thou that art full of grace, the Lord is with thee" – which represent the moment of Christ's Incarnation – are embossed in Latin in the gold background. Martini and Memmi have created a pious image of sophisticated grace, using the opulence of the materials as an expression of spiritual splendour. As the Virgin shies away from the divine messenger, the naturalism of the scene is also clear.

PATTERNED MOTIFS
Martini was the first to use elaborate motif punches, rather than ring punches (below right), to decorate gold. As this detail shows, the haloes are inscribed with compasses or dividers and the gold is stamped with motifs. These patterns would shimmer in candlelight, giving a supernatural aura to the image.

The checks on the Angel's cloak emphasize its natural movement

The vase holds white lilies – a symbol of the Virgin's purity

The simulated marble floor enhances the rich effect

MAKING PUNCHED DECORATION
After the painting surface has been gilded (beaten gold leaf is laid over bole, a reddish-brown clay, and polished with a burnisher), punched designs are made by holding the punch upright on the burnished gold leaf, then tapping sharply but softly with a hammer (left). The punch should produce an indent in the gold and its underlying preparatory surface, without breaking the film of thin gold leaf.

PUNCHING TOOLS
The Sienese developed the taste for punched gold ornament in panel painting, and exported tools to Florence. While modern punching tools (left) are made of cast metal, all but the simplest early Italian punches seem to have been cut by hand, so that each was unique.

Renaissance Florence

THE WEALTHY CITY REPUBLIC of Florence nurtured some of the most spectacular accomplishments of the Renaissance. Despite the loss of half its population in the plagues of 1340 and 1348, and the turbulence of warfare, popular uprisings, and political conspiracies, 15th-century Florence prospered. Governed as an independent commune by rich merchant families and guilds (trade associations; p. 63), the city was renowned for its tradition of liberty, its financial and political astuteness, and its superior craft skills. Under the patronage of the famous Medici family (1434–94), the easy exchange of ideas between politicians, artists, and scholars continued, and Florence entered a period of unrivalled cultural vitality. Pride in its achievements manifested itself in an ambitious building programme, which aimed to make the city a model of beauty, order, and harmony.

VIEW OF FLORENCE
By the 15th century, Florence had absorbed the territory of many of its hostile neighbours, becoming the largest city in Europe. Surrounded by beautiful Tuscan countryside and protected by fortified walls, it nevertheless led a precarious existence. This map shows how the city is divided by the River Arno and is dominated by the dome of the Cathedral, which was to become a symbol of Florence's civic fortitude.

A marble bust of Brunelleschi, acclaimed as the "most famous Florentine architect"

THE CATHEDRAL DOME

Brunelleschi (right) designed a dome (1420–36) to crown the 14th-century Cathedral of Santa Maria del Fiore: it had remained incomplete, with a huge octagonal opening that posed enormous constructional problems. Although Brunelleschi went to Rome with the sculptor Donatello (p. 14) to study classical buildings, the dome is largely Gothic in character, built around a self-supporting masonry of eight main ribs.

Ribs are visible on the exterior

The lantern admits light into the interior; it was completed after Brunelleschi's death by Michelozzo

ENGINEERING INNOVATION
Brunelleschi invented a hoisting machine with pulleys (above): the masons no longer had to carry materials to the dome's staggering heights. Citizens were forbidden to hitch a ride on this unique machine.

The complexity of the 14th-century Cathedral contrasts with the simple, harmonious structure of the dome

PHILIPPI BRVNELLESCHI
FLORENTINI ARCHITECTI
CELEBERRIM EFFIGIES
OB·AN·SAL·M·CCCCXLIIII

BUST OF BRUNELLESCHI
Filippo Brunelleschi (1377–1446) first trained as a goldsmith, like his Florentine contemporaries, Donatello and Ghiberti (pp. 14–15). He turned to sculpture but, after losing a competition for the new Florence Baptistery doors (p. 14) to Ghiberti, devoted himself to architecture. The huge dome of Florence Cathedral is his towering achievement.

CHURCH OF SANTO SPIRITO, RIGHT AISLE
In 1436, Brunelleschi designed the Church of Santo Spirito, which movingly expresses the ideals of the Early Renaissance. Here, the lofty Corinthian columns and niches faithfully copy antique examples. These Roman elements are combined in simple new geometric relationships, based on human proportions (pp. 30–31), to give a sense of order, space, and serenity.

THE TORNABUONI CHAPEL

The prosperity and prestige of Florence's ruling families lay at the heart of the city's artistic activities. This chapel, in the great Dominican Church of Santa Maria Novella, was owned by the Tornabuoni family, who were linked to the illustrious Medici family through marriage. Giovanni Tornabuoni, the head of the Medici bank and treasurer to Pope Sixtus IV, chose the popular painter Domenico Ghirlandaio (1449–94) to decorate his chapel with scenes from the lives of the Virgin and St. John the Baptist.

A Latin inscription adorns the classical temple

The Angel Appearing to Zacharias (detail)

DOMENICO GHIRLANDAIO
1485–90; fresco

Ghirlandaio's frescoes in Santa Maria Novella give a vivid insight into the political life of Florence in the late 15th century. This detail shows how a religious event has been transformed into a hymn to Florence's prosperity. Here, members of the Tornabuoni family are portrayed as "witnesses"; portraits of the leading scholars of the Tornabuoni/Medici circle appear elsewhere. The temple behind bears the inscription (detail, above left) of the fresco cycle's completion: "In the year 1490, when the most glorious city, renowned for its wealth, victories, arts, and architecture, enjoyed salubrity and peace."

SYMBOLS OF THE COMMUNE

The medieval Palazzo Vecchio, which was the seat of the Republican government, is adorned with the coats of arms of the commune (above), city wards, and public offices.

The famous symbol of the Florentine lily (centre) was adopted in the latter part of the 13th century.

This 16th-century plaster bust of Machiavelli is by an unknown Florentine master

DANTE STANDING BEFORE FLORENCE

Domenico di Michelino; 1465; fresco
Florence's proud literary tradition dates from the time of the poet Dante (1265–1321), the narrative writer Boccaccio (1313–75), and the scholar and poet Petrarch (p. 6). This painting of Dante with his famous poem, *The Divine Comedy*, was placed in Florence Cathedral after the town of Ravenna had refused to return the poet's precious remains.

THE POLITICIAN MACHIAVELLI

The political writer Niccolò Machiavelli (1469–1527) witnessed the fall of the Florentine Republic in 1512. He had been an active member of the Republican regime, and spent his enforced retirement analysing the egotistical ways of humanity and the ruthless realities of political power. Machiavelli also insisted on the pre-eminence of Florence by championing Florentine Italian as the language of the whole of Italy. These ideas were eloquently expressed in his writings, the most famous being *The Prince*.

Early Renaissance sculpture

In FLORENTINE SCULPTURE of the early 15th century, the rapid pace of innovation was dictated by an atmosphere of open competition and rivalry. The independent associations of masters that represented the trades and professions – the guilds – vied with one another in their decoration of civic buildings. The sculptors based their style – especially in the field of relief, when the sculpture projected from a background – on Graeco-Roman sculpture, the most visible evidence of their ancient heritage. The North, however, led the way towards a more majestic figure style, infusing sculpted forms with lively realism. The Florentine sculptor Lorenzo Ghiberti (1378–1455) even claimed that his style was derived from the work of a goldsmith in Cologne.

THE MOSES FOUNTAIN
*Claus Sluter; 1395–1406; height:
1.83 m (6 ft); wood with polychrome*
This huge work by the Burgundian sculptor Claus Sluter (d.1405/6) was once part of a cloisters. The massive, individualized figures reveal a realism new to Northern art.

Ghiberti's Baptistery doors

Ghiberti spent most of his career working on two pairs of doors for Florence's Baptistery, a church opposite the Cathedral. He had just completed the North doors (1401–25), drawing on his expertise as a goldsmith to master bronze techniques, when the Guild of Cloth Importers commissioned a second set (1425–52). Now Ghiberti stunned his contemporaries with his new compositional and perspective skills (pp. 28–29).

THE GATES OF PARADISE
Ghiberti's East doors (these are replicas – the originals have been removed to a museum) were so admired by later sculptors that Michelangelo called them the "Gates of Paradise". There were originally meant to be 28 panels illustrating Old Testament episodes, but Ghiberti reduced these to ten by skilfully incorporating several events into each scene.

FRAMED PORTRAIT
This wry self-portrait of Ghiberti looms out of one of the small roundels in the frame of the door.

JOSEPH IN EGYPT
This panel of *Joseph in Egypt*, from Ghiberti's doors, illustrates his striking use of three or more planes of perspective in one scene. The graceful figures mostly inhabit the front plane; some move through the immense architecture in the middle plane; and the background dissolves into a convincing spatial vista (in the manner of Donatello's relief, below right).

THE SCULPTOR'S ART
This detail forms the right-hand portion of a relief by the Florentine sculptor Nanno di Banco (c.1374–1421). It shows a stonemason carefully measuring proportions and a sculptor chiselling a figure, with his mallet ready on one side. The relief is at the base of a niche dedicated to the Stonemason's Guild on the Florentine guild Church of Or San Michele. Each of the guilds – from the Linen Drapers to the Armourers – was given its own niche, which it had to fill with a statue. Due to the threat of invasion, the guilds were urged to fulfill this obligation: the sculptures were completed within 20 years and display the skills of the foremost sculptors of the day.

St. George

DONATELLO *1415–17;*
height: 2.09 m (6 ft 10 in); marble

Donatello (c.1386–1466) established his reputation as the greatest sculptor in Italy with this statue of *St. George*, made for a niche on Or San Michele. St. George was the patron saint of the Guild of Armourers and Swordmakers, in whose niche he stood. The figure is infused with a dramatic inner life (notice the furrowed brow and sensitive features) and a dynamic alertness: each muscle is taut, the shield rests momentarily on its point, and the hands have the tension of readiness in repose.

Drill holes at the back of the head indicate that St. George once had a helmet

The armour is carefully described

The corroded metal of the sword's socket is just visible

MISSING WEAPON
The clenched left hand still holds a socket, which is stained with corroded metal (detail, above). This shows that the saint was originally equipped with a metal sword (fashioned by the swordmakers, Donatello's patrons). Pointing out at the viewer, into the street, it would have enhanced the statue's realistic impact.

This panel is shown in detail below

CANTORIA
Luca della Robbia; 1431–38; 3.28 x 5.60 m (10 ft 9 in x 18 ft 4 in); marble
This beautiful marble *Cantoria* (Italian: "Singing Gallery"), by Luca della Robbia (1400–82), was one of the most popular works of the Early Renaissance. It was originally positioned above the door of the North Sacristy in Florence Cathedral, overlooking the high altar. Children and infants, who sing and play music, are presented in a panelled frieze. They illustrate verses from Psalm 150, in which God is praised "with the sound of the trumpet ... with stringed instruments and organs".

DETAIL OF CANTORIA
Although Luca della Robbia's relief panels are based on Roman examples, they have a natural charm and vivacity that reflect Florentine tastes of the time. Della Robbia has created an ideal of grace through the flowing lines of the draperies and the smooth polish of the sculpted forms. His *Cantoria* faced another by Donatello, in which the figures seem almost violent by comparison.

ST. GEORGE AND THE DRAGON
Donatello's most revolutionary innovation lies in the marble relief beneath the statue of *St. George*. In conventional relief sculpture, rounded figures were raised from a level back panel (far left). Donatello, however, has flattened his forms and made the background dissolve into space, light, and air.

SCULPTING TOOLS
The carving tools of the sculptor have changed little over the centuries. Chisels were struck with a mallet: the pointed chisel chipped off large pieces of stone, shaping the figure, and the flat chisel was used on the surface.

The courtly style

At the end of the 14th century, Gothic art north and south of the Alps acquired an international flavour, as communications between European courts improved. A new style, which is known as "International Gothic", flourished all over Western Europe in the period between 1380 and 1430, spreading from centre to centre as trade routes multiplied and commercial wealth increased. It was shaped by the aristocratic taste for elegance, ornamental variety, and decorative splendour. The beautifully observed natural detail of Gothic art was often incorporated into more realistic settings, but was still represented within an overall decorative scheme. Nurtured in its main centres of Paris and Burgundy – where the grace and delicacy of French manuscript illustration fused with the imagery and style of both Sienese and Flemish painting – the fashionable courtly style also had a persuasive influence in northern Italy.

DECORATIVE TAPESTRY
International Gothic, with its ornamental style, was especially suited to the decorative nature of tapestry. The "Devonshire Hunting Tapestries" (detail of *The Bear and Boar Hunt*, c.1430–35, above) are some of the few surviving early 15th-century examples.

THE WILTON DIPTYCH
c.1395; each wing: 53 x 37 cm (21 x 14½ in); tempera on panel
This diptych (p. 25), which may have been King Richard II's private altarpiece, shows him being presented to the Virgin and Child by King Edmund, King Edward the Confessor, and St. John the Baptist – the angels wear the white hart of King Richard's livery. The grace of the figures and delicate detail are typical of the new style.

Interior of the diptych

Exterior of the diptych

The right wing shows the white hart of Richard II

The arms of Edward the Confessor are impaled on King Richard II's Royal coat of arms

APRIL (FROM "LES TRES RICHES HEURES DU DUC DE BERRY")
The Limbourg brothers (Pol, Herman, and Jean) worked for the Duke of Berry, one of the greatest collectors of illuminated books, who owned more than 150 sumptuous manuscripts. They decorated a Book of Hours (a religious book offering prayers and meditations appropriate to each hour, day, or month) for him, the famous *Très Riches Heures*. This full-page illustration from the *Très Riches Heures* is a perfect example of International Gothic elegance, showing sinuous figures, clothed in rich draperies, in a deep naturalistic landscape.

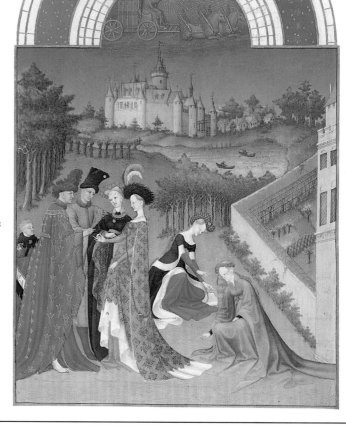

Adoration of the Magi

GENTILE DA FABRIANO *1423;*
3.00 x 2.82 m (9 ft 10 in x 9 ft 3 in); tempera on panel

This flamboyant work was painted by the northern Italian artist Gentile da Fabriano (c.1370–1427) for one of the wealthiest citizens in Florence, Palla Strozzi. Gentile had been employed by the Venetian government and the princely courts of northern Italy: Strozzi now expected him to use his courtly style to display his own wealth and rank. The altarpiece was made for the Sacristy of Santa Trinità, the chapel where the clergy dressed in their gorgeous ceremonial attire. The ornate frame is matched by the splendour of the Magi (the Three Kings) and their retinue, who wind though the hills to pay homage to the newborn Christ. Their finery – and the sheer abundance of natural detail – vividly evoke the joyous nature of the occasion.

Tiny painted panels in the side of the frame are filled with fruits and flowers

EXPERIMENTS WITH LIGHT
This scene, from the predella panel of Gentile's *Adoration of the Magi*, may show the journey of Mary, Joseph, and the child Christ from Bethelehem to Jerusalem (although it is often described as depicting the Flight into Egypt). Here, Gentile has abandoned the conventional gold background (seen in the sky of the main panel) and has created an atmospheric landscape with a real blue sky. The soft, natural light emanating from the gilded sun marks the beginning of a new phase of naturalism in Italian art. Light illuminates the distant buildings, gentle hills, and the fruit and foliage.

GOLD DECORATION
Glittering gold ornament is raised from the surface of the painting so that it looks like solid gold. This has been achieved by applying gold leaf over a moulded layer of gesso (a plaster-like material, used to prepare panels for painting).

17

The Brancacci Chapel

MASACCIO (1401–28) WAS THE FIRST GREAT Italian painter of the Early Renaissance. Building on the legacy of Giotto (pp. 8–9), and embracing the innovations of his Florentine contemporaries – Donatello's expressive sculpture (p. 15) and Brunelleschi's perspective system (pp. 28–29) – he developed a sober, monumental style of profound naturalism. Christened Tommaso, he was nicknamed Masaccio ("clumsy Tom") because of his lack of worldliness and his slovenly appearance. His art, too, is plain and unadorned, showing little interest in the intricate detail of the International Gothic style, and concentrating instead on the physical and spiritual bulk of his figures. Masaccio's most famous work is in Florence: an unforgettable fresco cycle in the Brancacci Chapel, Santa Maria del Carmine, executed alongside works by his collaborator, Masolino di Panicale (active 1423–47).

THE RAISING OF TABITHA
Masolino di Panicale; c.1425;
2.25 x 5.98 m (7 ft 5 in x 19 ft 7 in); fresco
The Brancacci Chapel frescoes were commissioned by the wealthy merchant and diplomat Felice Brancacci in 1423, and work began the following year. In 1428, the fresco cycle was left unfinished, to be completed in 1481–82 by Filippino Lippi. Masolino's elegant style, with its flamboyant use of the new perspective system, has suffered by comparison with the weighty naturalism of Masaccio. In this fresco, the two Biblical episodes of the Healing of the Cripple (on the left) and the Raising of Tabitha (on the right) appear within a contemporary Florentine setting. The cobblestones, which become smaller the further away they appear, lead the eye into a townscape filled with detail.

The Tribute Money

MASACCIO *c.1425; 2.25 x 5.98 m*
(7 ft 5 in x 19 ft 7 in); fresco
Masaccio and Masolino seem to have worked together from the beginning, dividing the spaces equally between them. The two most famous scenes, *The Raising of Tabitha* (above right) and *The Tribute Money* (right), are at the same level on facing walls. Both are painted from the same viewpoint, with the ground sloping upwards, so that we feel that we can enter the scenes. Masaccio's "modernity" can be seen in the intensity and gravity of the poses and facial expressions; in the way the viewer's attention is focused by the perspective construction (all the receding lines of the architecture lead to Christ's head); and in the unifying light, which gives such airiness to the landscape and such substance to the realistically draped figures.

SCULPTURAL INSPIRATION
Masaccio was influenced by the sculpture of Giovanni Pisano (active c.1265–1314), son of the famous Pisan sculptor Nicola Pisano (active c.1258–78). The Pisani revived the heroic forms of classical sculpture, and also inspired Giotto's figure style. The head of Adam in Masaccio's *Expulsion* (detail, below left) was probably inspired by Giovanni's vivid portrayal of the damned on the pulpit of Pisa Cathedral (1302–10; left).

SOULS IN TORMENT
Like Giotto, Masaccio uses the physical posture of his figures to reveal the emotions of their souls. Eve's abandoned suffering is expressed through the pitiful angle of her head, Adam's more private torment through the way he stoops in shame, shading his face with his hands. As he leans forward, so she throws her head backwards, her mouth open in a cry of anguish.

Pisano's figure borrows its pose from the familiar ancient type known as the "modest Venus"

The weight of the figure is taken on one leg, following the example of antique statues (p. 48)

EVE'S ANCESTOR
The figure of Eve in Masaccio's *Expulsion* (right) is similar to Giovanni Pisano's figure of *Temperance* on the pulpit of Pisa Cathedral – which is itself based on a classical figure type.

THE EXPULSION
Masaccio; c.1427; 208 x 88 cm (82 x 34¾ in); fresco
Masaccio's harrowing scene of the expulsion of Adam and Eve from the Garden of Eden shows the expressive force and directness of his style. An angel drives the sinners into the harsh, barren world, where the light mercilessly exposes their guilt and despair. Masaccio's composition is beautifully balanced within the narrow format. The forward movement, dictated by the gesture of the angel, is firmly anchored by the strong vertical running from the heads of Adam and Eve to their heels. The muscular tension of Adam's body, and the fluidity of Eve's, were inspired by a contemporary relief.

THE TEMPTATION
Masolino di Panicale; c.1425; 208 x 88 cm (82 x 34¾ in); fresco
Masolino's *Temptation*, in which Eve is tempted by the devil in the guise of a serpent, faces Masaccio's *Expulsion* across the entrance to the Brancacci Chapel. The contrast between the two couples – Masolino's is graceful and courtly, Masaccio's is heavy, contorted, and emotionally charged – reveals the differing artistic visions of the two painters. The figures of Masaccio are stark, but their rounded forms fill the space they stand in; they seem to embody the essence of humanity, while Masolino's have an air of detachment.

Flemish naturalism

I<small>N THE</small> N<small>ORTH</small>, the spirit of Flemish art was transformed by the dramatic naturalism and monumental style of sculpture from Burgundy (p. 14). The Tournai master Robert Campin (c.1375–1444) was the first to flesh out his holy figures and place them in "real", everyday interiors, filled with sacred symbols. The famous Bruges artist Jan van Eyck (active 1422–41) rendered the minute detail of such settings with breathtaking realism, his revolutionary oil technique allowing him to create subtle effects of light, space, and texture. The spiritual essence of a scene was displayed with similar technical virtuosity by Rogier van der Weyden (c.1339–1464). His international renown was exceeded only by that of Hugo van der Goes (active 1467–82), who united Van Eyck's naturalism with penetrating studies of humanity.

A MAN IN A TURBAN
Jan van Eyck; 1433; 33.3 x 25.8 cm
(13 x 10¼ in); oil on panel
This picture, which is still in its original frame, is often identified as a self-portrait of Van Eyck. The frame is inscribed with his modest motto, "As I can", at the top (this may be a pun on his name: "As Eyck can"), and "Jan van Eyck made me on 21 October 1433" along the bottom. The astonishing sense of the sitter's presence is created through contrasts of light and shadow: the face (complete with stubble) seems to project out of the frame, emerging dramatically from the dark background.

THE ARNOLFINI MARRIAGE
Jan van Eyck; 1434; 81.8 x 59.7 cm
(32¼ x 23½ in); oil on panel
This double portrait shows Van Eyck's mastery of natural light effects, from the clear daylight filtering through the window to the convex mirror on the back wall, which reveals light streaming through a doorway (detail, below). The picture is thought to mark the marriage of an Italian merchant, Giovanni Arnolfini (a resident of Bruges), to Giovanna Cenami. Van Eyck seems to have invested ordinary items with deeper meanings: the chair, for instance, is carved with the figure of St. Margaret, the patron saint of childbirth.

In medieval symbolism, a lighted candle represents God

SYMBOLIC LIGHT
The brass chandelier (detail, right) reveals not only the delicacy of Van Eyck's light effects, but also a lone candle burning in a room filled with daylight. It is often interpreted as the "marriage candle", traditionally lit in the home of newly-weds.

PAINTING IN OIL
These details show the intricate effects that can be achieved using oil paint (colours blended in a medium of oil, such as linseed or walnut). Van Eyck refined the technique, using the transparency of certain oil colours to build deep, jewel-like tones and blending the slow-drying paint with his fingertips.

Detail of the slashed sleeve, from Van Eyck's *The Arnolfini Marriage*

Detail of brocade underskirt, from Van der Weyden's *The Magdalen Reading* (above right)

MIRROR IMAGE
This detail shows how the mirror frame is decorated with scenes from Christ's Passion (his suffering and Crucifixion) and Resurrection. The mirror itself reflects two more figures – visitors, or even marriage witnesses. The artist's inscription above – "Jan van Eyck was here, 1434" – suggests that he may be one of them!

THE MAGDALEN READING

Rogier van der Weyden; c.1445; 61.6 x 54.6 cm (24¼ x 21½ in); oil on panel
This fragment from an altarpiece shows Mary Magdalen, one of the holy women, reading in an ordinary room. Van der Weyden has included certain details, such as the delicate carvings of the wooden cupboard and the glinting tacks in the floorboards. The subtle handling of light, however, which illuminates the whites of Mary Magdalen's head-dress and draped Bible, focuses the viewer's gaze on her demure figure.

SYMBOLS OF REPENTANCE
The Magdalen is identified by her "attribute" of the ointment jar, an object that is always associated with her. The jar (detail, above) contains costly myrrh, which she used to anoint Christ. She reads from a precious illuminated Bible (right) that matches her rich attire, and symbolizes her new life of holy works. Once a courtesan, she now personifies repentance – inviting sinners to restore themselves by her example.

ADORATION OF THE SHEPHERDS (PORTINARI ALTARPIECE)

Hugo van der Goes; c.1476–78; 2.53 x 5.86 m (8 ft 3 in x 19 ft 2 in); oil on panel
The huge *Portinari Altarpiece*, by the Ghent master Hugo van der Goes, was commissioned by the Medici representative in Bruges, Tommaso Portinari, for his chapel in Sant'Egidio, Florence. Its arrival in 1483 caused a great stir among Italian artists. The central panel depicts the Nativity and the Adoration of the Shepherds, while the wings include portraits of the Portinari family and their patron saints. The extreme realism of the aged male saints and coarse-featured shepherds is matched by the naturalism of the landscape.

PORTRAITS FROM LIFE
The portraits of the Portinari children have been used to date the altarpiece. They and their mother were painted from life, directly onto the wings (c.1477–78). But it seems that Tommaso's head was painted on a separate surface before the wings were started (because he was leaving for Italy), and was later glued into place.

MEANING IN THE FLOWERS
The natural still life in the foreground of the central panel is symbolic: the scarlet lily, for instance, represents the red blood of Christ; the purple columbines symbolize the sorrows of the Virgin; and the sheaf of grain refers to Christ's birthplace, Bethlehem (Hebrew: "house of bread").

The artist's craft

THE ARTIST'S ROLE in the Renaissance was much more varied than that of artists today. Artists learned their craft in a busy workshop, run by a master who obtained the commissions they worked on. They ground colours, prepared wooden panels for painting, gilded with gold leaf, and mastered a range of techniques. The work undertaken ranged from altarpieces, and grand murals in churches, town halls, and palaces, to small images for prayer, civic portraits (often sent as diplomatic gifts), painted furniture, festival decorations, book-covers, and stage sets. Style and subject-matter were often dictated by the function of a picture, as well as the surroundings in which it was to be seen.

THE CRAFTSMAN'S HANDBOOK
Cennino Cennini's *The Craftsman's Handbook* (c.1400) provides a vivid account of early Italian fresco and egg tempera techniques (p. 63). Egg tempera was the most popular medium for 15th-century Italian panel paintings.

ST. LUKE PAINTING THE VIRGIN AND CHILD
Follower of Quinten Massys; 1510–30;
113.7 x 34.9 cm (44¾ x 13¾ in); oil on panel
Pictures of artists at this time usually depict St. Luke, the patron saint of painters. They also give an idea of the tools and materials used by Renaissance artists. This Flemish panel shows the saint, who is identified by his symbol of the ox, painting a portrait of the Virgin. The fine brushes and the stick, which he uses to steady his hand, reveal the painstaking nature of his technique.

CONTRACTS
For most major commissions, the patron – who paid for a work of art – detailed requirements in a contractual agreement. This contract, for an altarpiece of 1453 by the artist Enguerrand Quarton, insists that the finest pigments be used, and specifies the subject-matter and medium.

PAINT SUPPLIERS
The apothecaries, whose medicinal art is shown in this Latin manuscript illustration, were closely identified with painters (in Florence, they belonged to the same guild – the Guild of St. Luke – along with the spice merchants and doctors). They were one of the main suppliers of pigments – colours in powdered form, from natural earths, minerals, plants, or animal stuffs – used by artists. The most costly colours of ultramarine blue and vermilion red were often supplied by religious orders.

PAINTING SUPPORTS
Most Renaissance artists worked on wooden panels. These were made from poplar, oak, silver fir, and other suitable woods: this one, part of the reverse of a painting of St. Paul, is made of white poplar, which was the preferred support in Italy. After 1450, canvas, which had been used largely for temporary festival decorations and theatrical scenery, became more common. In 16th-century Venice (pp. 44–45), canvas was used for large-scale works because it could be rolled up and transported easily. It also resisted the city's damp conditions better than fresco or panel.

The Medici emblem of three feathers in a ring appears on the parapet in the centre of the painting

The Virgin's bedstead is decorated with inlaid wood designs

THE BIRTH OF ST. JOHN THE BAPTIST
Giovanni di Paolo; c.1427; 30.8 x 36.4 cm (12 x 14¼ in); tempera on panel

Religious images were the mainstay of the artist's workshop: they ranged from full-blown altarpieces (which were placed on church or chapel altars) to small paintings of the Virgin and Child, designed for private devotion in the home. This panel, by the Sienese painter Giovanni di Paolo (active 1425–83), is one of five scenes from the life of St. John the Baptist, which once formed the predella of an altarpiece. It shows St. Elizabeth lying exhausted in bed after giving birth to St. John the Baptist. The head and foot of the bed are decorated with painted panels, as was the custom in Giovanni di Paolo's day (see above).

THE ANNUNCIATION
Fra Filippo Lippi; c.1448; 68.6 x 152.4 cm (27 x 60 in); tempera on panel

This panel by Fra Filippo Lippi (c.1406–69), with its sweet domestic setting, was designed for the "*camera*" – an intimate chamber that was used as both drawing room and bedroom. It is one of two half-moon-shaped pictures by Lippi, which were probably placed above beds in the Medici Palace. Panels of inlaid wood (Italian: "*intarsie*") were also popular in such rooms, as were beautiful fabrics and wall-hangings. In wealthy households, pride of place was given to heavily woven Netherlandish tapestries, which were more costly than paintings; in *The Annunciation*, the "carpet" of foliage and flowers deliberately imitates tapestry patterns.

WEDDING CHEST
A number of the narrow, horizontal Italian paintings that survive, such as Uccello's *Hunt* (p. 28), once decorated wedding chests (Italian: "*cassoni*") or their back panels (Italian: "*spalliere*"). The chests often sported stirring narratives illustrating manly virtues – and matching images of female virtues. This *cassone* is one of a pair created for a society wedding of 1472, and still has its *spalliera* intact.

THE YOUTHFUL DAVID
Andrea del Castagno; c.1450; 115.6 x 76.9 cm (45½ x 30¼ in); oil on leather, on panel

Painters had to work on all types of commissions, including decorations for festivals and pageants. The great Florentine master Andrea del Castagno (c.1419–57) painted this leather shield, which was probably carried in jousts. Appropriately, the winner of the battle, David, stands over the slain Goliath.

Images of devotion

DURING THE RENAISSANCE, there was a huge demand for religious images. The number of altarpieces increased as they were commissioned by orders of monks and friars, guilds, the confraternities (lay associations devoted to religious cults or works of charity), and wealthy citizens, while small, ready-made pictures were bought by pious individuals. In Italy, whole chapels were often frescoed with cycles illustrating stories from the Bible (pp. 8–9; pp. 18–19). In the North, stained glass, and the great portal sculptures of figures and reliefs around church doorways, served a similar purpose. Much of the imagery was dominated by the lives of the saints – their martyrdom had inspired the early Church – and the cult of the Virgin. Altarpieces depicting the crucified Christ were also common, providing an appropriate backdrop to the ritual celebration of mass.

HOLY RELICS
Martyred saints were often adopted as patrons. Churches were named after their patron saint, and all altars contained relics (believed to be pieces of the saint's body or clothing), which were objects of veneration. This reliquary from San Domenico's in Bologna, Italy, contains St. Dominic's skull.

PREACHING SERMONS
Popular preachers like Fra Roberto Caracciolo (shown in this Florentine woodcut of 1491) made the teachings of the Church accessible to an illiterate public. Fra Roberto infused holy stories with drama, explained their significance, and indicated the appropriate emotional response. The gestures and actions, made recognizable by preachers, were used in a similar way by painters to provoke pious emotions.

THE DEPOSITION
Fra Angelico; c.1440–45; 275 x 285 cm (108¼ x 112¼ in); tempera on panel
The Italian painter Fra Angelico (1387–1455) was a Dominican friar, and placed his art at the service of his order. This altarpiece, painted for the Strozzi family chapel in the Florentine Church of Santa Trinità, is radiantly coloured to shine in the chapel's gloom.

THE VIRGIN AND CHILD WITH SAINTS FRANCIS AND SEBASTIAN
Carlo Crivelli; 1491; 175.3 x 151.1 cm (69 x 59½ in); oil on panel
This altarpiece, by the Venetian painter Carlo Crivelli (active 1457–93), was painted for a Franciscan church. It shows St. Francis (on the left) and St. Sebastian – who is pierced with the arrows of his martyrdom – flanking the Virgin and Child. Crivelli's altarpiece was commissioned by the widow Oradea – and her portrait is included. She is the tiny figure peeping out from behind St. Francis's leg (detail, right). Such portraits of the benefactor ("donor" portraits), however, were often shown the same size as the holy figures (p. 21).

GESTURES
These two details from Fra Angelico's altarpiece illustrate how gestures are used to tell a story and reveal particular emotions. One man crosses his hands in an expression of humility (above right). The kneeling foreground figure (right) commends the viewer to Christ's mercy, inviting him or her to pay similar homage to Christ. His right hand is held to his chest in a gesture of reverence.

The Deposition
ROGIER VAN DER WEYDEN
c.1435; 220 x 262 cm (86½ x 103 in); oil on panel

Van der Weyden emphasized the spiritual elements of the scenes he painted: this moving episode shows Christ being lowered from the cross by Nicodemus (a secret disciple) and Joseph of Arimathea. The Virgin, in a faint, is supported by St. John the Evangelist, whose rhythmic, stooping posture is mirrored by that of the grief-stricken Mary Magdalen opposite. The figures are compressed into a shallow space, much like the sculpted wooden shrines (below) that decorated Gothic churches.

This was once the central panel of a triptych (see below)

MUTUAL SUFFERING
The Virgin's pale hand, limp with grief, is movingly juxtaposed with the mutilated hand of her crucified son.

ARCHERS' BOWS
Tiny crossbows in the tracery refer to the Archers' Guild, which commissioned the altarpiece.

ST. WOLFGANG ALTARPIECE
The Austrian sculptor and painter Michael Pacher (active 1462–98) produced elaborate carved, painted, and gilded altarpieces. This massive work (1471–81) has a sculpted, gilded shrine at its centre; is topped with pinnacles and painted figures; and is closed with painted wings – as is the predella panel. Decorated with scenes from the *Life of the Virgin* and the *Legend of St. Wolfgang*, it is shown here in the Church of St. Wolfgang, near Salzburg. Pacher himself supervised its installation there, as his contract with his patron, the Abbot of Mondsee, had specified.

ALTARPIECE FORMATS
Altarpieces take various forms: the diptych (left) has two hinged panels that close like a book; a triptych (above), three panels – the wings close; and a polyptych, several panels (such as Duccio's *Maestà*, p. 10). There is also the single rectangular panel, the "*pala d'altare*", an innovation of the Italian Renaissance.

Classical inspiration

THE 15TH-CENTURY ENTHUSIASM for the remains of ancient Rome followed in the wake of the rediscovery of classical manuscripts in the Middle Ages. Mythological and classical themes gained in popularity and artists studied the monuments and sculptures that surrounded them. A growing awareness of Italy's cultural origins was also stimulated by the continual unearthing of statues and artefacts. The ancient reliefs, which had inspired Gothic artists with their natural forms, became a treasure trove of dramatic poses and stylistic ideas. While artists like Donatello and Andrea del Verrocchio (1435–88) revived classical types, from the colossal equestrian monument to the small bronze statuette, the northern Italian master Andrea Mantegna (1431–1506) combined his broad interests in archaeology (which included the recording of classical inscriptions) with artistic invention.

CHRIST BEFORE PILATE
Jacopo Bellini (1400–70/1), the father of Giovanni (pp. 34–35), used antique motifs in a free and imaginative manner. This page from his volume of drawings reflects the fashion for setting New Testament subjects in their Roman context: here, Christ is brought to trial before Pontius Pilate beneath a triumphal arch (see left).

The equestrian monument embodies the Roman ideal of public virtue

THE ARCH OF TITUS
The triumphal Arch of Titus (c.81 A.D.) stands in the Forum in Rome. The reliefs on such arches, which commemorated imperial processions and battles, were avidly copied by artists and antiquarians. The arches themselves often appear in fanciful guise in the backgrounds of paintings.

CLASSICAL TRANSLATIONS
The humanist scholar Lionardo Bruni was a driving force behind the translation of many classical Greek works into Latin in the 15th century. This manuscript page begins his account of the ancient Punic War (in which the Romans defeated the Carthaginians), based on the work of the Greek Polybius. It was made for the library of the Gonzaga family in Mantua, and is adorned with their crest and arms of 1433.

GATTAMELATA
Donatello; 1445–53; height: 3.70 m (12 ft 2 in); bronze
Donatello's huge equestrian portrait of the mercenary captain Gattamelata revives one of the grandest and most technically ambitious forms of ancient sculpture – the monumental equestrian bronze. It emulates the antique equestrian statue of Marcus Aurelius in Rome (late 2nd century A.D.), which had survived because it was thought to show the Christian emperor Constantine. Donatello's horse is directly adapted from one of the four ancient gilded horses on the facade of San Marco in Venice.

THE INTRODUCTION OF THE CULT OF CYBELE AT ROME ("THE TRIUMPH OF SCIPIO")
Andrea Mantegna; 1505–6; 73.7 x 268 cm (29 x 105½ in); monochrome on canvas
This episode from the Punic Wars shows the Romans bearing the goddess Cybele in the form of a stone, and her bust. Prophecies had decreed that the Carthaginians would only be expelled from Italy if the goddess was carried from Asia Minor to Rome and received by the city's worthiest man; Scipio Nasica was chosen. Mantegna painted the scene (commissioned by the Cornaros, who claimed to be descendants of the Scipios) to look like a Roman cameo. The figures – some of which are based on actual Roman reliefs and statues – appear against an exquisite simulated marble background.

HERCULES AND ANTAEUS

Antonio del Pollaiuolo; c.1470s;
height: 45.7 cm (18 in); bronze

This small-scale bronze of wrestling figures by the Florentine artist Antonio del Pollaiuolo (active 1457–98) imitates antique examples. In his portrayal of Hercules and Antaeus engaged in violent conflict, Pollaiuolo was one of the first to present a mythological subject "in the round". It is so dramatically styled and anatomically detailed that it almost demands to be rotated so that its multiple viewpoints can be admired. The idea of displaying figures from contrasting viewpoints was also practised by Pollaiuolo in his paintings to show that two-dimensional works could equal sculpture in their realism.

Antaeus's agonized expression and taut arm show the body at breaking point

Flying limbs animate the surrounding space

Hercules's calves ripple with straining muscles

DEATH OF ORPHEUS (AFTER MANTEGNA)

Although the Northern interest in antiquity was initially based in classical writings, woodcuts of Italian works in the antique style were copied in 15th-century workshops. Similarly, Dürer (pp. 40–41) looked to Italian artists rather than directly to the antique. His fascination with Italy's artistic heritage was fostered by his friendship with the Nuremberg humanist Willibald Pirckheimer. This, together with his determination to master the art of engraving, led Dürer to make drawings after famous mythological prints by Mantegna. Dürer's pen drawing of 1494, after a lost Mantegna engraving, shows the poet Orpheus being clubbed to death by the women of Thrace, and reflects Dürer's own vigorous response to the scene.

PUTTO AND DOLPHIN

Andrea del Verrocchio;
c.1470s; 67 cm (26½ in);
bronze

This winged infant was made for the centre of a fountain at the Medici country villa of Careggi, a place for leisure and intellectual pursuits. Its light-hearted charm reflects the relaxed atmosphere that was associated with country villas of classical times.

The "invention" of perspective

LINEAR PERSPECTIVE – a mathematical system for representing three-dimensional space on a flat surface – was devised in Florence in the early 15th century. Brunelleschi (p. 12) demonstrated its principles, but a fellow architect and writer, Leon Battista Alberti (1404–72), was the first to formulate rules that the artist could follow. In Alberti's system, the picture surface is imagined as an "open window" through which a painted world is seen. He showed how a perspective "chequerboard pavement" (like a squared floor) is created within the picture space – in which the receding parallel lines (the orthogonals) represent visual rays connecting the spectator's eye to a spot in the distance. This spot, on which all the rays converge, is known as the "vanishing point", and is positioned directly opposite the spectator's viewpoint. The single viewpoint meant that the artist could now control and focus the way the spectator looked at his picture.

ETIENNE CHEVALIER WITH ST. STEPHEN
Jean Fouquet; c.1450; 93 x 86 cm (36½ x 33¾ in); oil on panel
In Northern painting, perspective was judged by the eye, rather than dictated by theoretical rules. Jean Fouquet (c.1420–c.1481), France's leading painter and illuminator, visited Italy and became fascinated with the construction of spatial settings. In this panel, he uses his favoured diagonal format, with the diminishing squares of the "chequerboard" floor tiles (a common device) and the spacing between the architectural columns providing the main perspective clues, along with the wonderful manipulation of light.

ALBERTI'S DEVICES
As a perspective aid, Alberti devised his grid or "veil" – a transparent material divided into squares by coloured threads and stretched over a frame. This device, illustrated in this treatise by Dürer (1525), was placed between "the eye and the object to be represented" so that the object could be drawn to scale.

THE HUNT IN THE FOREST
Paolo Uccello; 1460s; 73 x 177 cm (28¾ x 69¾ in); tempera and oil on panel
The Florentine artist Paolo Uccello (1397–1475) was so enamoured with the new "science" of perspective that, according to Vasari, he used to stay up all night searching for vanishing points. This obsession can be seen in his paintings, which playfully experiment with all manner of objects that lead the eye back into space. Here, horses charge towards an off-centre vanishing point, with carefully placed logs pointing the way.

UCCELLO'S FRAMEWORK
This perspective analysis of Uccello's *Hunt* shows the importance of the "horizon line" in perspectival construction. This horizontal line, drawn across the painting at the vanishing point, represents both the viewer's eye-level and the far distance. It creates the sense of a three-dimensional space, by making us assume that the forest floor (which slopes upwards) is flat. We imagine the tiny running figures to be roughly the same height as we are, because if one of the figures was positioned at the very front of the picture, his eye-level would be on the horizon line, like ours. The orthogonals of the "pavement" are marked by the bases of the standing tree trunks, which lead our eye to the vanishing point near a far tree (encircled by hounds).

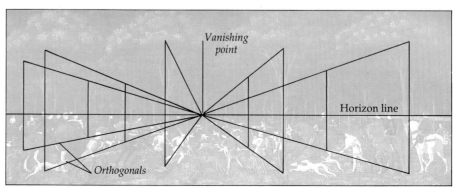

Vanishing point

Horizon line

Orthogonals

Adoration of the Kings

BRAMANTINO
*c.1498; 56.8 x 55 cm
(22½ x 21¾ in); oil on panel*

The Milanese painter
and architect Bramantino
(c.1465–1530), a pupil of
Bramante (p. 51), wrote
a treatise on perspective
(now lost) and had an
unusually complete grasp
of perspective method.
His *Adoration of the Kings*
gives us a remarkable
insight into the way
Alberti's system worked
in practice, because the
numerous constructional
lines – of the receding
perspective grid – are
actually ruled and incised
in the preparatory gesso
(see artwork, below left).
Bramantino used this
perspective framework
to scale his figures and
architecture and position
them correctly in space,
but he also took pains
to disguise the textbook
rigidity of the construction.

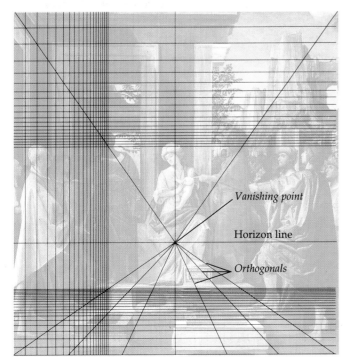

Vanishing point

Horizon line

Orthogonals

**BRAMANTINO'S
PERSPECTIVE PAVEMENT**
Bramantino divided the base
of his picture into six equal
units, incising orthogonals
from these points to a central
vanishing point just below the
Virgin's knee. Lines were also
incised from the top corners
down to this vanishing point.
Bramantino then continued the
horizon line – drawn through
the vanishing point – out to
the left of the picture space (on
a separate work surface), to a
point representing the chosen
viewing distance. From here,
Bramantino drew lines to the
units at the base of the picture.
Where these lines intersected
the left edge, Bramantino made
a series of marks, from which
he incised the horizontal lines
of his pavement. This framework was, however, used
imaginatively: three containers
placed in the foreground lead
the eye into the distance subtly.

*Two extra
steps, cloaked
in shadow in
the painting,
rise behind the
Virgin's seat*

FIGURES ON THE DAIS
The grid units – the "tiles" of the perspective
pavement – provide a ground plan for all the
objects in the painting. This plan is so precise
that computer graphics can "erect" the stepped
dais, and the main figures positioned upon it,
three-dimensionally. It can even show the dais
from a side viewpoint (above). This suggests
that Bramantino may have employed a three-
dimensional model with movable figures
when working out details such as the lighting.

Harmony and beauty

AN ANCIENT IDEAL of beauty, based on mathematical and musical notions of harmony and proportion, was revived in Italian Renaissance circles. The theorist and architect Alberti explained in *De Re Aedificatoria*, his treatise on architecture of 1485, that "Everything that Nature produces is regulated by the law of harmony, and her chief concern is that everything should be perfect. Without harmony this could hardly be achieved, for the critical sympathy of the parts would be lost." This perfect harmony, the balance of which is destroyed if anything is added or subtracted, can be created by the artist or architect through a careful arrangement of component "parts". Using the flawless logics of mathematics, he can ensure that the parts of a painting or building are proportionally related to the whole – and thus form the beauty of ideal proportion. The human body itself, the "noblest living form", was regarded as a model for God's universe, and the measure from which the wider world could be constructed.

BUILDING PROPORTIONS
Alberti's facade for the Rucellai Palace in Florence (1455–58) consists of three storeys of equal height, divided by pilasters (the flat upright pillars) that support entablatures (the horizontal elements). The pilasters are topped with capitals, which are as wide as the central entablatures are tall.

MAN, THE MEASURE OF ALL THINGS
Leonardo's famous drawing, *Vitruvian Man* (c.1487), illustrates a classical formula devised by Vitruvius. It is simply explained by the mathematician Luca Pacioli, who often worked with Leonardo: "Having considered the right arrangement of the human body, the ancients proportioned all their work, particularly the temples, in accordance with it. In the human body they discovered the two main figures without which it is impossible to achieve anything, namely the perfect circle and the square." Spread-eagled, the man fits into a circle; with feet together and arms outstretched, he fits into a square.

ON HUMAN PROPORTION
Dürer was inspired by his reading of a treatise by the Roman architect Vitruvius (1st century B.C.), and studies of proportion by Leonardo da Vinci (far left; pp. 36–37), to write his own work on the subject (1528; left). He divided figures of different heights into sections, and carefully calculated their measurements as fractions of the total length – as "parts" of the "whole".

PERSPECTIVE ARRANGING
This drawing of a *Wellhead* is from a perspective treatise by Piero della Francesca (c.1415/20–92), the great painter and mathematical theorist. Pacioli (Piero's pupil) said that "nine out of ten words" of this treatise were, in fact, on proportion, the art of arranging things. Here, Piero shows how a three-dimensional object can be constructed from a plan and logically positioned in space. The proportions are mathematically calculated with the utmost precision.

The Baptism of Christ
PIERO DELLA FRANCESCA
1450s; 167 x 116 cm (65¾ x 45¼ in); tempera on panel

The monumental grandeur and apparent simplicity
of this altarpiece derives partly from the fact that it
uses exact proportional arithmetic and is constructed
around pure geometrical shapes (below). Piero valued
"the placing of profiles and contours in their proper
places in proportion" in an image. He places the
figure of Christ, thought to be the most perfect of
"human" forms, at the very centre of the work,
making him half as tall as the panel is high.

MATHEMATICAL DIVISIONS
Piero's composition is divided into halves (passing
through the figure and face of Christ) and thirds (on
which the tree, Christ, and St. John the Baptist are
placed); even the relationship between the height of
the panel and its width is in a ratio of about 3:2. Two
circles, one with the dove of the Holy Spirit at its
centre, the other with the tips of Christ's fingers, make
mathematical and symbolic sense of this arrangement.

THE HARMONIC SCALE
This woodcut of 1480 shows the theory of
Western musical harmony developed by the
mathematician Pythagoras (6th century B.C.).
The musical scale was divided into harmonic
intervals, which were expressed through
numbers. Its sequence – 6, 8, 9, 12 – and its
harmonic proportions (the interval between
6 and 12 is an octave, between 8 and 9 a tone)
were adapted by some painters and architects.

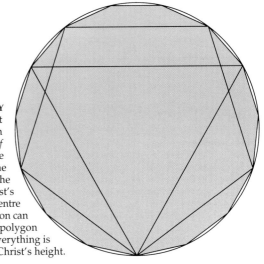

EUCLIDIAN GEOMETRY
It is thought that Piero used Euclid's ancient
formula for constructing a 15-sided polygon
as the mathematical basis for the *Baptism of
Christ* (which would be in the position of the
lower circle, above right). The wings of the
dove are arranged along the base line of the
upside-down equilateral triangle, with Christ's
right foot at its downward point. From the centre
of this, a circle, pentagon, and, finally, a polygon can
be generated. The length of each side of the polygon
is the unit of measurement around which everything is
constructed: it is exactly one-third of Christ's height.

Botticelli and mythology

THE CELEBRATED *Primavera* ("Spring") by Sandro Botticelli (1445–1510), a large imaginary scene depicting figures from ancient mythology, represents a new type of picture, prized in cultured Renaissance circles. It is the painted equivalent of a lyric poem, invoking the spirit of Venus, goddess of love and springtime, and inviting the viewer to enter her realm of perpetual beauty and abundance. The work was probably commissioned sometime after 1478 for the Medici residence known as the *"case vecchie"* in Florence, which had been inherited by Lorenzo de' Medici's young wards – it was originally fitted into the wainscoting above a daybed in one of the ground-floor rooms. Vasari mentions that such room decorations were executed with wondrous skill and "poetic invention", and showed jousts, tournaments, festivals, and other spectacles of the time. There is no doubt that this painting is linked to the sumptuous Medici pageants (it may actually commemorate one of them), for which Botticelli painted fabrics and banners. These pageants reflected the rich literary interests of Lorenzo's scholarly circle: drawing on both the vivid classical descriptions of ancient rustic festivals and rites (in Latin verse), and the ornate imagery of Tuscan love poetry and chivalric romance.

ANCIENT INSPIRATION
The group of three figures on the right in the *Primavera* is derived from an ancient myth related in Ovid's *Fasti* (title page, above). In this, the Greek nymph Chloris explains how she became "queen of flowers". As she roamed in spring, Zephyr (the west wind) pursued and raped her, but later married her – making her the goddess of spring, whom the Romans called Flora. Zephyr gave her "a fruitful garden ... filled with noble flowers".

EMBLEM OF THE MEDICI
The Medici emblem of *palle* (Italian: "balls"), from their coat of arms, is subtly alluded to in Botticelli's grove of orange trees, with its mass of rounded golden fruit (right). Other trees have symbolic meanings – the myrtle in the centre, for instance, is sacred to Venus.

SEEDS OF FERTILITY
Seed clusters rise around the feet of Mercury, the messenger of the gods. He is shown (on the extreme left) stirring the clouds with his wand, which is adorned with dragon-like snakes (symbols of fertility). His role has perplexed art historians – Botticelli may have included the god because he presided over the seed-dispersing spring winds.

Primavera

SANDRO BOTTICELLI *c.1478;*
203 x 314 cm (80 x 123½ in); tempera on panel
Botticelli's rustic idyll centres on the figure of Venus, who raises her hand in a traditional gesture of welcome. She is attended by her son, Cupid, the god of love, who takes aim with his flaming arrow. Her handmaidens, the Three Graces – goddesses of charm, grace, and beauty – dance at one side. They are shown "with hands interlocked ... smiling and youthful, clad in loosened transparent gowns", just as the ancient author Seneca had described them. He was writing about a lost classical painting in which Mercury stands alongside the Graces. In the Renaissance, Alberti recommended Seneca's description as an imaginative treatment of a subject that painters could emulate.

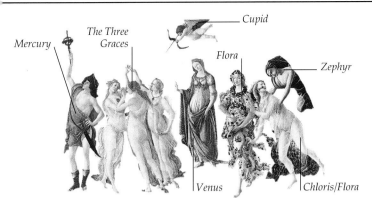

Mercury — *The Three Graces* — *Cupid* — *Flora* — *Zephyr* — *Venus* — *Chloris/Flora*

FIGURES FROM ANCIENT MYTH
The nine figures in Botticelli's painting originate in ancient Greek and Roman myth. They are almost life-size in scale and are usually identified as above. All are associated with the ancient festivals of springtime, particularly the "Floralia" (the festivals of Flora). Venus symbolizes the season's fertility, while Mercury and Flora are associated with the month of May.

THE REBIRTH OF CHLORIS
As the goddess of flowers tells of her rustic origins, her mouth, in Ovid's words, "breathes the roses of spring". Botticelli has shown Chloris with flowers streaming from her mouth, as if she is being transformed into Flora at Zephyr's embrace. The figure next to her is often identified as the "reborn" Flora – her cult was in existence in Rome at an early date. She has also been interpreted as the "Hour" (ancient spirit) of spring.

> **"** *Ove madonna volge gli occhi belli, senz'altro sol questa novella Flora fa germinar la terra e mandar fora mille vari color di fior novelli.* **"**

> **"** Wherever my lady turns her beautiful eyes, with no other sun does this new Flora cause the earth to germinate and to put forth the thousand various colours of the new flowers. **"**

Lorenzo de' Medici

THE POETRY OF SPRING
The sonnets of Lorenzo (an extract is quoted and translated above) use the season of spring as a metaphor for the fertile power of love – here, his "lady" is identified as "Flora", or spring. An acclaimed poet from his circle, Politian (1454–94), draws on the same traditional imagery; the presence of the beloved lady can transform even the most desolate place into a flowering springtime paradise, as seems to be the case in Botticelli's vision.

FESTIVAL COSTUME
Flora's gown may be based on the white dress "painted with roses and flowers and greenery" worn at a Medici tournament of 1475 and commemorated in Politian's verses.

MAY DAY FESTIVALS
This woodcut shows Lorenzo de' Medici at the "*Calendimaggio*" celebrations in Florence. This popular May Day festival had its origins in the ancient Floralia. Its dancers, like Botticelli's figures, gave welcome to the spring "that makes man fall in love" (Politian).

SCHOLARLY ADVISOR
Artists were sometimes advised by experts – Politian may have shaped Botticelli's "invention". The classical scholar Guarino da Verona, portrayed in this medal, was consulted on details of this painting (right) by Cosimo Tura (active 1451–1495).

AN ALLEGORICAL FIGURE
Cosimo Tura; 1450s; 116.2 x 71.1 cm (45¾ x 28 in); oil and tempera on panel
This classical figure, painted for the "*studiolo*" (a private room for intellectual recreation) of Lionello d'Este of Ferrara, is full of erudite literary symbols that may never be deciphered. It probably shows one of the Nine Muses, who presided over the arts in ancient myth.

The rise of landscape

THROUGHOUT THE 15TH CENTURY, there was a growing interest in "landscape" – the depiction of natural scenery in painting. While earlier artists had used a stock formula of rocky outcrops and stylized trees to emphasize the grouping of their figures, painters now filled their backgrounds with a charming variety of narrative detail, or created deep vistas to demonstrate their new perspective skills. Instead of the costly gold grounds that were so common in altarpieces, Italian patrons began to specify "landscapes and skies" in their commissions, wishing to acquire something more individually tailored and tasteful. This fashion for decorative landscape detail was imported from the North, where there was a strong tradition of landscape in illuminated manuscripts and tapestries. Northern artists also developed the technical means to create miraculously natural effects of light and distance, using the oil medium to bathe their landscapes in atmosphere.

THE ENTOMBMENT
Dieric Bouts; c.1450–60; 90.2 x 74.3 cm (35½ x 29¼ in); glue size on linen
The Netherlandish painter Dieric Bouts (c.1400–75) used landscape to set a contemplative tone. Here, the figure composition is gently pushed to the left, drawing the eye towards the infinite landscape on the right. The natural background also includes traditional narrative details that are appropriate to the theme: a rocky cliff, symbolic of death, surmounts Christ's lifeless head, while the fertile scenery beyond hints at rebirth and salvation (details, below). Bouts's approach is unusual in that he values the landscape for its own sake, as a place for meditation. His painting technique, in which pigments mixed in glue are absorbed by the linen cloth support, heightens the soft effect (although some of the original depth of colour has been lost).

Detail of rocky landscape

Detail of fertile landscape

The Agony in the Garden

GIOVANNI BELLINI *c.1465; 81.3 x 127 cm (32 x 50 in); tempera on panel*
The Venetian artist Giovanni Bellini (c.1435–1516) quietly revolutionized Italian landscape painting. His portrayal of *The Agony in the Garden*, which is closely based on a painting of the same subject by Mantegna, his brother-in-law (above right), is remarkable for its unifying light and all-enveloping atmosphere. Day is breaking, and the rosy light of dawn softens the lines of the gently swelling landscape. Christ kneels in prayer on a cushion of rock, which slopes upwards to form a simple altar, while his disciples slumber on the barren ground. As Christ prays, awaiting his arrest, the soldiers are already approaching (led by the traitor Judas) under a departing swathe of dark, rippling cloud. Bellini's landscape lyrically expresses the dawning of Christianity.

THE AGONY IN THE GARDEN
Andrea Mantegna; c.1460; 62.9 x 80 cm (24¾ x 31½ in); tempera on panel
The compressed geological landscape of Mantegna's *Agony* is painted with the precision of a miniaturist. In contrast to Bellini, he has chosen to stress the human agony of Christ's ordeal as he contemplates his imminent Crucifixion. The suffering of Christ is expressed in minute natural details, such as the writhing roots of a fallen tree and the axe marks in its bark (on the right). An awareness of the value placed on illusion by the artists of antiquity probably provided the impetus for Mantegna's inventive realism: the rock seems to shape itself into a shrouded corpse at Christ's knees – a "fantastic invention", worthy of the great classical painters.

VIEW OF THE ARNO VALLEY
Leonardo's landscape studies combine scientific observation with the force of the imagination. This early drawing of the Arno valley in Tuscany represents a real view, dated to a particular day (5 August 1473). Yet its vast sweep transforms this objective record, unique in its time, into an image of the artist's creative powers. Leonardo had noted how the artist, "as lord and creator", can perceive the world's enormous variety "in a single glance".

ST. JEROME IN A ROCKY LANDSCAPE
Ascribed to Joachim Patenier; 1515; 36.2 x 34.3 cm (14 x 13½ in); oil on panel
The Flemish painter Joachim Patenier (d.1524) was the first artist to specialize in landscapes. This fantastic rocky landscape is surveyed from a high viewpoint – a Northern innovation that had become popular in Italy (as in Leonardo's drawing, above).
The panoramic grandeur of the scenery may also reflect the new conception of the world that followed Columbus's discoveries.

TEMPESTA
Giorgione; c.1505; 83 x 73 cm (32½ x 28¾ in); oil on canvas
With the emergence of the private collector, the actual subject-matter of a painting became less defined. Connoisseurs desired more decorative works that would be "pleasing to the eye", would harmonize with their interests (pastoral poetry or music, for instance), and would suit the intimate atmosphere of their private apartments. Small landscape paintings with pastoral or erotic themes first became fashionable in Venice, in the circle of Giorgione (1476/8–1510). His *Tempesta* (Italian: "Storm") is one of the first Italian paintings to be described as a "landscape". Giorgone uses his oil technique, in which light areas emerge from a dark background, to add to the twilight poetry of the scene.

The genius of Leonardo

LEONARDO DA VINCI (1452–1519) was a man of unique gifts, whose fertile imagination produced images of unequalled vitality and beauty. His drawings and notebooks (pp. 38–39) reveal that "the divine art of painting" was just one of a mass of activities that absorbed him. He was also skilled in anatomy, botany, sculpture, architecture, music, optics, and much else besides. His genius, as Vasari relates, was such that he confounded "the boldest minds". Yet Leonardo "envisaged such subtle, marvellous, and difficult problems that his hands, while extremely skilful, were incapable of ever realizing them". That is why so many of his paintings and projects were never completed, and why his fellow citizens and artistic rivals were prepared to queue in procession to see a wondrous "cartoon" (full-size preparatory drawing), similar to the one opposite, by his hand.

YOUTHFUL GRACE
This detail of *David* by Leonardo's master, Verrocchio, suggests the renowned physical beauty of the young Leonardo.

FLORENTINE MASTER
Born in Vinci, near Florence, Leonardo trained in the busy workshop of Andrea del Verrocchio (p. 26). Leonardo finished his apprenticeship in 1472, when he was entered as an independent master in the register of the Guild of St. Luke (above).

VERROCCHIO'S EXAMPLE
Verrocchio, a Florentine goldsmith, sculptor, and painter, was also one of the most gifted draughtsmen of his day, as his eloquent drawing of a girl with elaborately dressed hair demonstrates. He taught his pupils to make exquisite studies from nature, to draw forms in perspective, and to study the nude in various postures. Leonardo was fascinated by the intricate hairstyles that were then so fashionable; his works include similar portraits of girls with plaited tresses, and the intertwining forms of "many designs of knots".

FACE OF AN ANGEL
Leonardo's varied light effects can be seen in this detail. He made a scientific study of light and shadow in nature and also experimented with the light-reflective properties of translucent layers of oil paint. The lustre of each hair is delicately picked out, but he avoids the strong, shiny reflections often used by Northern artists – on the whites of the eye, for instance. Instead, a soft light plays over the angel's ethereal features.

MONA LISA
Leonardo; c.1503–6; 77 x 53 cm (30¼ x 20¾ in); oil on panel
The beguiling beauty of this famous portrait derives as much from the haunting mountainous landscape as from the enigmatic Florentine woman who inhabits it. The veiled ambiguity of her smile gives the painting its timeless appeal. Seated high on her balcony, she is at once welcoming and remote.

STUDIES OF NATURE
The studies of plants that appear in the foreground of *The Virgin of the Rocks* show Leonardo's botanical interests. Although the flowers are conventionally symbolic, Leonardo's understanding of their growth and structure is revealed in the movement he has imparted to them. They seem to stir with an inner life.

THE VIRGIN OF THE ROCKS
Leonardo; c.1508; 189.5 x 120 cm (74½ x 47¼ in); oil on panel
This, Leonardo's second version of *The Virgin of the Rocks*, was installed in the centre of an altarpiece in the Milanese Church of San Francesco in 1508. Certain details were left unfinished, such as the angel's left hand and Christ's back. The image is based on a tale in which the infant Christ and St. John the Baptist meet in the wilderness, where John lives as a child hermit, looked after by an angel. Here Christ (on the right) blesses John. Leonardo has given the scene a mysterious beauty by veiling everything in shadow.

Leonardo uses a complex pyramid of overlapping and intertwining forms to express the interaction between his holy figures. The Virgin is half-seated on the lap of her mother, St. Anne, while Christ's twisting pose unites them. The arc formed by his body links with the Virgin's arm and Anne's shoulder to form a sacred circle. These geometrical rhythms also underlie the way the other forms balance and flow into one another. The figures are compressed into a small space, to powerfully concentrate the overall effect of the cartoon.

LEONARDO'S SIGNS

The emotions of the figures are revealed through their facial expressions and gestures. Christ's right hand is precociously raised in blessing, while with his other hand he cradles his cousin's chin. The face of the Virgin, suffused with light, is gently indulgent and filled with grace. Her mother's expression is smudged in smoky shadow, but her finger, pointing upwards, suggests the divine foreknowledge that lies behind her strange smile.

SMOKY TECHNIQUE

The *sfumato* (Italian: "smoky") technique – in which outlines are softened and shadows blurred – was introduced into painting by Leonardo. Although areas of rough outline have been left visible in this preparatory drawing, the *sfumato* effects are clear in the more fully worked upper portion of the composition – particularly in the faces. No doubt the distant mountain landscape and the pebbles in the foreground would have been veiled and softened in the final work; in Leonardo's oil paintings, the outlines all but disappear in a mist of atmospheric colour.

The Virgin and Child with St. John the Baptist and St. Anne

LEONARDO *c.1507–8; 141.5 x 104.6 cm (55¾ x 42 in); black and white chalk on tinted paper*

Leonardo's only surviving cartoon may be a variant of a lost drawing that was exhibited in 1501 in Florence: it made such an impression on his contemporaries that some, like the young Michelangelo, tried to mimic Leonardo's astounding compositional skills (in the *Doni Tondo*, p. 55). This later cartoon may be related to an altarpiece on the same theme, made for King Louis XII of France. The design is full size, but it has never been transferred to panel – there are no prick-holes in the drawing surface.

PRICKED CARTOON
This detail from Raphael's *Cartoon for an Allegory* shows how holes are pricked along the outlines to transfer a design. The cartoon was placed over a panel and dusted over with powdered charcoal, so that the powder went through the prick-holes and stained the surface beneath.

Leonardo's explorations

THE VOLUMINOUS NOTEBOOKS of Leonardo – two of which were discovered as recently as 1965 – provide a fascinating record of his endless inventiveness and the complexity of his genius. They are written in reverse, in his famous "mirror" writing, a style that naturally suited his left-handedness, and are illustrated with explanatory drawings. Alongside his scientific explorations of every facet of perspective, colour, light and shade, and human anatomy, there are designs for flying machines, mathematical puzzles, ball-bearing mechanisms, steam cannons (of the type later used in the American Civil War), and even musical instruments. Like other artists of the time, Leonardo adapted his skills as an architect to the profitable area of military engineering, canal building, and weapon design. His letter of introduction to Lodovico Sforza, the Duke of Milan, explains how he can contrive collapsible bridges, machines for draining trenches, siege equipment, armoured cars, and multi-barrelled guns (ancestors of the modern machine gun). At the end of the letter, he briefly details his peacetime abilities as an architect, sculptor, and painter! His writings lay down a challenge to future generations, "to pursue and invent things anew".

LEONARDO AND MUSIC
An outstanding performer on the *lira da braccio* (above), Leonardo made his own instrument, as well as new types of drums and a keyboard.

DRAWING OF A DELUGE
Leonardo's series of *Deluge Drawings* (c.1515) – which show cataclysmic visions of rain, waves, foam, and whirlpools – are linked to his scientific researches into the dynamics of water, and how its flow has "changed the face and the centre of the world". Leonardo was mesmerized by the primeval power of water, which has the potential to wreak universal havoc: "The waters destroy the mountains, fill the valleys, and would reduce the world to perfect sphericalness if they could."

HUMAN ANATOMY
Leonardo planned a treatise on anatomy and carried out dissections of over 30 bodies. Here, he has made a detailed anatomical study of the muscles of the arm. Leonardo regarded the body as the ultimate machine, using its components to solve intricate mechanical problems such as the wiring of a keyboard (based on the tendons of the hand) or the design of a musical recorder (based on the upper larynx).

The crank and pulley mechanism

HUMAN FLIGHT
This model, made by James Wink in 1988, is based on designs for a flying machine that Leonardo made almost 500 years earlier (above right). It also draws on Leonardo's later researches into bird-like winged structures, which focus on mechanical details such as the working of the joints. Leonardo never quite resolved how the leg movements of the person flying should synchronize with the motion of the wings. The modelmaker's solution was to incorporate a crank and pulley system, of the type that Leonardo experiments with elsewhere. When the model is in operation, the wings flap with extraordinary bird-like grace, but its weight (the materials are those specified by Leonardo) keeps it firmly on the ground.

The wings were to be operated by foot pedals

THE GREAT BIRD

This *Design for a Flying Machine* is from one of Leonardo's manuscripts of 1488. A later collection of notes, dated 1505, is devoted exclusively to flying contraptions and "the flight of birds". Leonardo planned to launch his craft from Monte Ceceri ("Mount Swan"), near Fiesole: "The great bird will take its first flight on the back of the great swan, filling the universe with amazement, filling all writings with its renown and bringing glory to the nest in which it was born." Earlier he had suggested that "the machine should be tried over a lake ...".

CHARACTER STUDIES

Leonardo's *Profiles of an Old Man and a Youth* (c.1495) reveals his interest in the science of physiognomy. This involved interpreting the external "signs of faces" that, as Leonardo explained, "show in part the nature of the men, their vices and complexions". Leonardo often carried a sketchbook so that he could capture types, from the beautiful youth to the elderly grotesque.

The model's wing span is 11 m (36 ft)

The skeleton structure had to be supported by thick struts

CASTING A BRONZE SCULPTURE

This drawing is one of a series detailing the construction of a monumental bronze horse for Lodovico Sforza. Here we see the iron grid-work of the head and neck, which will reinforce the plaster or clay of the outer mould.

The model, made to Leonardo's specifications, weighs a massive 295 kg (650 lb)

WEAPONS OF DESTRUCTION

Leonardo called war "beastly madness", but nevertheless devised some of its deadliest, most ingenious weaponry. This drawing of *Military Machines* (1487) shows a design for a scythed chariot (top), together with an armoured vehicle (bottom), shaped like a cockroach, that fires from all around its rim. Leonardo also claimed to have invented the most deadly mortar machine in existence: "... the ball in the centre bursts and scatters the others with fires in such time as is needed to say an Ave Maria!"

Dürer's pioneering role

THE PAINTER'S FATHER
Ascribed to Albrecht Dürer; 1497;
51 x 40.3 cm (20 x 16 in); oil on panel
Only the face of this portrait of
Dürer's father is held to be by
Dürer. The features are given
sharpness and clarity by the
emphasis on line and detail.

THE GERMAN PAINTER and printmaker Albrecht Dürer (1471–1521) was
determined to elevate the status of art in the North and gain international
recognition as an "artist-painter", rather than a craftsman. He approached
these twin tasks with almost missionary zeal: travelling to Italy to seek
instruction from Italian Renaissance masters; studying languages and
cultivating princes to enhance his social standing; making engravings and
woodcuts of unprecedented size and complexity (which were copied by
artists all over Europe); and writing important treatises on perspective
and human proportions. The son of a goldsmith, Dürer's intellectual and
artistic ambitions were fuelled by his godfather, the printer and publisher
Anthony Koberg, and his friendship with the famous classical scholar
Willibald Pirckheimer, who had prompted his study of Italian Renaissance
ideas. But it was, above all, Dürer's technical inventiveness and consciousness of his own originality that gave
him such a pivotal role in the history of European art.

THE FOUR APOSTLES
Albrecht Dürer; 1526; each panel: 214.6 x 76.2 cm
(84½ x 30 in); oil on panel
Dürer's mature style was dominated by Italian ideals of
monumentality and grandeur. These two panels, his last
paintings, also reveal his involvement with the new
religious ideas of the Reformation (pp. 42–43). Each apostle
represents one of the four human temperaments (for
example, Paul, shown full-face, is melancholic), which
suggest different and individual ways of experiencing God.

THE GREAT PIECE OF TURF
Albrecht Dürer; 1503; 41 x 31.5 cm (16 x 12½ in); watercolour and gouache
Dürer studied every detail of nature, approaching even
a piece of turf with an analytical eye. This watercolour was
executed at the same time as animal studies, which were
recorded with similar microscopic exactitude. Such delicacy
of observation was translated into an increasingly refined
engraving technique (right), in which many details can only
be truly appreciated by looking through a magnifying glass.

VIEW OF THE ARCO VALLEY
Albrecht Dürer; 1495; 22.5 x 22.5 cm (8¾ x 8¾ in); watercolour
This watercolour landscape of Arco, on Lake Garda, was executed on Dürer's return from Italy in 1495. Here, the strict accuracy of the individual parts of a view – Dürer's enduring interest – has been sacrificed for the harmonious unity of the overall scheme.

Master printmaker

Dürer's prints show a supreme mastery of their respective mediums. Dürer pushed the technique of line engraving – which had originated in the 15th century in the goldsmith's workshop – to its limits. The line engraving (right) is created by gouging lines in a copper plate with a sharp tool known as a "burin". Ink is then sunk into the grooves and the plate pressed onto damp paper. For the ancient technique of the woodcut (below right), the wooden block was cut away around the sinuous lines of the design, leaving the image raised and ready to be inked (below).

KNIGHT, DEATH, AND THE DEVIL
Albrecht Dürer; 1513; 25 x 19 cm (10 x 7½ in); engraving
This master engraving shows how meticulously and expressively Dürer handled the burin. He used tightly spaced strokes, dots, and networks of dense parallel lines to create velvety shades and tones, as well as atmosphere. The subject is the active power of Christian faith – embodied in the steadfast knight armed with spiritual weapons, who clings to the rocky path of virtue even when threatened by the spectre of Death or the Devil.

ST. JEROME IN HIS STUDY
Following his apprenticeship in the studio of Michael Wolgemut, Nuremberg's leading painter and book illustrator, Dürer found work designing woodcuts. This frontispiece was made for a collection of St. Jerome's writings, which was published in Basel in 1492 – unlike the later *Knight, Death, and the Devil*, which was designed as a work of art in its own right. The block from which it was printed (left) was cut rather crudely by a professional woodcutter (it is now riddled with wormholes). Within a few years, Dürer was performing the majority of the cutting himself; later, he trained members of his busy workshop in his own dynamic style of woodcutting.

The Reformation

THE RADICAL RELIGIOUS BELIEFS of the German Martin Luther (1483–1546) – which brought about the division of Western Christendom – altered the nature of sacred art. As part of the Holy Roman Empire, Germany was subject to the Catholic Church in Rome, and received papal reprimands for "the foulest abominations and filthiest excesses" of some of its people. Luther resented this emphasis on sin and punishment, and, in 1521, he came into direct conflict with the Papacy over the sale of "indulgences" – documents bought for cash that could be offered in place of doing penance. He believed that salvation could only be granted by the grace of God, not through human works. As Luther's ideas spread, some painters abandoned images of hell and damnation, and art began to reflect the spirit of the new Protestant faith.

THE TEMPTATION OF ST. ANTHONY
Matthias Grünewald; 1515; 250.2 x 92.7 cm (98½ x 36½ in); oil on panel
This scene by the German artist Matthias Grünewald (c.1460–1528) appears on an inner wing of his *Isenheim Altarpiece*, which was painted for an Antonite Hospital Order. The story of their patron, St. Anthony, vividly illustrates the medieval belief that the soul could only achieve grace by actively resisting the Devil. Here, his suffering is paralleled by that of the diseased figure on the left.

THE TEMPTATION OF ST. ANTHONY
Hieronymus Bosch; c.1505–10; 132 x 119.3 cm (52 x 47 in); oil on panel
The Northern artist Hieronymus Bosch (c.1450–1516), an orthodox Catholic, had eminent Catholic patrons. He lived in an age beset by anxieties: plague was rife, as was religious and social turmoil, and people believed in physical manifestations of evil, such as witches. An astrological prediction of 1499 had stated that the world would end in 1524: this central panel of Bosch's triptych reveals his pessimism. The kneeling saint in the centre is surrounded by temptresses and demons, who personify evil planetary influences and human folly.

St. Anthony's writings are read by a bestial priest

A parody of the Virgin and Child on the Flight into Egypt

BOSCH'S INVENTIVE IMAGERY
Some of Bosch's images (details, above and right) are adapted from motifs in 15th-century astrological engravings, or earlier illuminated manuscripts. Animal snouts, for instance, appear as literal embodiments of a demonic or barbaric nature. The figure on the rat has a mermaid-like tail: mermaids were traditionally associated with evil.

ST. ANTHONY IN FRONT OF THE CITY
Dürer was profoundly influenced by Lutheran thought. In this engraving of 1519, he shows the hermit St. Anthony, believed to be the founder of the first monastic order, dressed in a monk's cloak and cowl, drawing moral strength from his inner struggles. This differs from the traditional depiction of him in the desert beset by weird creatures, as in Grünewald's panel (left). Although Grünewald had Lutheran sympathies, he also had Catholic patrons who saw Anthony as an instrument for the Devil to play on. In contrast, Dürer stresses the saint's personal relationship with God and the scholarly nature of his search for spiritual truth.

THE DANCE OF DEATH
A revival of the medieval theme of the Dance of Death also raised questions about the Catholic Church's authority. A skeletal figure of Death visits living individuals from every rung of the social ladder, showing that all humans are equal before death. The most famous example is the series of 40 woodcuts designed by Holbein and printed in 1538 (*The Astronomer* is shown left).

THE AMBASSADORS
Hans Holbein the Younger; 1533; 207 x 209.5 cm (81½ x 82½ in); oil on panel
This life-size double portrait by the German artist Hans Holbein (1497/98–1543) reflects the change in the intellectual climate brought about by the Reformation: the idea that humanity is no longer prey to its own folly, but has the power to achieve a virtuous state through the pursuit of knowledge. It shows Jean de Dinteville, the French ambassador, and Georges de Selves, Bishop of Lavour, in front of an array of instruments, used for learned pursuits. The strange object at their feet is a human skull shown in distorted perspective. When viewed from a certain angle, it takes a normal shape, serving as a *memento mori* ("reminder of death") and a warning against pride in knowledge for its own sake.

Death's face – a human skull

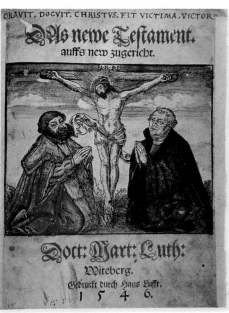

LUTHER'S BIBLE
Luther's insistence on returning to the original text of the Bible reduced the importance of the numerous tales that had sprung up around the lives of the saints and the Virgin. While outlawed and in hiding (under the protection of Frederick the Wise, the Elector of Saxony), he began his own German translation of the Bible, returning to the original Greek and Hebrew texts. The first Lutheran Bible was printed in 1534, and was hugely influential. Lay people now had access to its writings, along with the clergy. It received a new edition (left) in 1546 – the year of Luther's death.

The predella shows Luther preaching in front of a crucifix

REFORMATION ALTARPIECE, ST. MARIEN CHURCH, WITTENBURG
Lucas Cranach the Elder; 1547–52; centre panel: 120.7 x 81.3 cm (47½ x 32 in), wings: 120. 7 x 46.4 cm (47½ x 18¼ in); oil on panel
As court artist to Frederick the Wise, the German artist Lucas Cranach (1472–1553) was the "official" painter of the Protestant cause, although he continued to paint for Catholic patrons. He partly financed the first printing of Luther's Bible, and this altarpiece (completed by Cranach's son, Lucas the Younger) commemorates Luther's teachings.

The Venetian State

RENAISSANCE VENICE WAS one of the richest, most politically enlightened, and secure states in Europe. Her commercial prosperity rested as much on her mainland territories, which included Padua and Bergamo, as on her great sea empire – encompassing lands from Istria nearby, to Cyprus (acquired in 1489). Traditionally a sea-trading capital, where the exotic East mingled with the West, Venice became increasingly embroiled in the political wars in Italy (1494–1530), fought for control of the different states. She emerged proud and "inviolate", her strength due in large measure to the unique stability of her Republican constitution. In the absence of a court, artists benefited from State patronage. No one believed in the supremacy of Venice more than the Venetians themselves; they embellished their buildings and palaces, not just for personal prestige, but to enhance the greatness of the State.

VALUABLE CURRENCY
Artists were lured to Venice by the prospect of being paid in Venetian ducats, one of the strongest currencies on the international market.

THE ROLE OF THE SCUOLE
The Venetian "*Scuole*" – lay religious associations that administered charitable funds – were important patrons of art: the Scuola Grande di San Marco, which was managed by leading civil servants, employed three of Venice's leading artists for ceremonial duties and to decorate its headquarters (below).

After destruction by fire, the Scuola was rebuilt in 1485 with subsidies from the State

The lower part of the facade was redesigned by Pietro Lombardo

The Doge's Palace

THE DOGE LEONARDO LOREDAN
Giovanni Bellini; c.1501; 61.6 x 45.1 cm (24¼ x 17¾ in); oil and tempera on panel
Bellini has portrayed Leonardo Loredan, Doge from 1501 to 1521. The Doge was the elected ruler of the Republic. Like a modern monarch, he was head of state in name only, ruled for life (he was elected at a "mature" age), and had no political affiliations, other than those of his family. The Doge's Palace (above left) was decorated by the greatest painters of the day: Titian, Tintoretto (pp. 46–47), and Veronese (right).

Sansovino's great reputation temporarily plummeted in 1545, when one of the library's bays collapsed

The columns, arches, sculpted reliefs, and statues revive the splendour of Venice's ancient Roman past

The library is only two storeys high, so that it does not compete with the Doge's Palace facing it

THE MARCIANA LIBRARY
Since Venice was built on a lagoon, its buildings had to be supported by oak piles driven into the mud. Despite the limitations imposed by such an environment, famous architects were drawn to the capital. The Florentine Jacopo Sansovino (c.1486–1570) fled to Venice from the Sack of Rome in 1527 (p. 50) and was made architect to the Republic in 1529. His great library (1537–88) – which the architect Palladio described as "probably the richest building ever built from the days of the ancients up to now" – stands opposite the Doge's Palace on the Piazza San Marco.

Goods from the Middle and Far East were brought to the Mediterranean: this fragment from a world map of 1537 shows the lands in the Mediterranean for which the Venetian merchant galleys regularly set sail. Venice had acquired her sea empire for commercial reasons, to protect these trade routes.

Ultramarine (meaning "from across the seas") was shipped from Afghanistan

Ultramarine (violet-blue) Realgar (orange) Orpiment (yellow)

EXOTIC LUXURIES
Venetian trade in luxury goods from the East included exotic spices, such as nutmeg, mace, and, most importantly, pepper; dyes and pigments – the finest ultramarine and the orange and gold colours used in manuscripts (above); silks; jewellery; medicinal drugs; and ceramics.

Mace

Nutmeg fruit

Ground nutmeg Ground mace

Long pepper

Peppercorns

DECORATIVE RICHNESS
The Venetian taste for sumptuous fabrics, like this silk brocade (below), is reflected in the material splendour of Venetian painting, from the rich draperies, brocades, and decorative oriental rugs to the delight in stylized pattern and decoration (below left).

ENTHRONED MADONNA WITH SAINTS
Giovanni Bellini; 1505; 5.00 x 2.36 m (16 ft 5 in x 7 ft 9 in); oil on canvas
This altarpiece is still in the Church of San Zaccaria, Venice. It shows the Virgin and Child, absorbed in quiet meditation, surrounded by four imposing saints who occupy the same lofty, atmospheric space. This type of image, known as a *sacra conversazione* (Italian: "a holy communing", between the Virgin, Child, and saints), was given its most intimate, innovative form in Bellini's Venetian altarpieces. The music-playing angel enhances the mood of spiritual harmony.

THE MARRIAGE AT CANA
Paolo Veronese; 1563; 6.65 x 9.91 m
(21 ft 10 in x 32 ft 6 in); oil on canvas
Huge canvas pictures became a speciality in Venice, tolerating the damp conditions: this one was painted by Paolo Veronese (1528–88) for the Sacristy of San Giorgio Maggiore. The composition is so crowded with incidental detail – musicians, servants, jesters, dogs, guests in brocaded costumes – that it is difficult to notice Christ sitting quietly in the centre. This delight in festivity and everyday pleasures (dining, drinking, music, and conversation) is one of the most characteristic features of Venetian painting.

Titian, master of colour

TITIAN (C.1485–1576) WAS THE dominant painter of the Venetian Renaissance, and an artist of unparalleled international stature. He trained under Giovanni Bellini (p. 34), and later joined the workshop of Giorgione (p. 35): several of Titian's early paintings were once believed to be by Giorgione's hand. The novelty of Titian's approach, with its dynamic poses and bravura colouring, asserted itself in one of his first public commissions – the great *Frari Altarpiece*. This established his reputation as a startlingly original colourist, who employed colour rather than line as the main ingredient of his painting. It also revealed his ability to give an intensely physical form to spiritual rapture. His sensual style found its most exuberant outlet in his mythological paintings, including *Bacchus and Ariadne*, created for the Duke of Ferrara's castle, and the later erotic *poesie* ("painted poems"), made for King Philip II of Spain. Titian's patrons were wide-ranging: he was not only court painter to the Holy Roman Emperor, but was commissioned by the government and Church in Venice, the Gonzaga family from Mantua, and the Roman Farnese family of Pope Paul III. Titian's reputation ensured his position as Venice's rival to Florence's Michelangelo.

THE ASSUMPTION AND CORONATION OF THE VIRGIN
Titian; 1516–18; 6.9 x 3.6 m (22 ft 8 in x 11 ft 10 in); oil on panel
The colossal *Frari Altarpiece* was made for the high altar of the great Venetian Church of Santa Maria Gloriosa dei Frari. Titian's vision of the Assumption and Coronation, when the Virgin was raised up to heaven after her death and crowned, was so unconventional that the friars who commissioned the work were unsure whether to accept it. What no doubt disconcerted them were the emotionally charged poses, the boldness of the composition, and the rich sensuality of colour. The Virgin is virtually silhouetted by a blazing halo of light, witnessed by the Apostles, whose confusion and amazement is dramatized by deep shadows.

The complex, double-twisting pose of the Virgin is the first of its type in Venetian art

COLOUR TRIANGLE
Much of the impact of the *Frari Altarpiece* is created through the colour structure. The composition is divided into two large sections – a heavenly circle above, and the rectangular block of the Apostles below (in a shape that suggests the Virgin's sarcophagus). Titian uses a pattern of colour to unite the two areas: a tall triangle, formed by the vermilion robes of the two Apostles at the base, the Virgin's gown, and God's cloak, sweeps the eye up to the top of the altarpiece. He also used the finest pigments, juxtaposing them in contrasting patches of colour, which are carefully balanced to suggest that we are viewing the event in natural lighting conditions.

ARIADNE'S CONSTELLATION
The sparkling circle of stars in the sky (top left in the painting) symbolizes the moment when Bacchus tossed Ariadne's jewelled crown to the heavens.

FIGURES IN MOTION
The forward momentum, which culminates in the balletic leap of Bacchus in the centre, is set in motion by the crowd of figures behind him. The satyr, who brandishes a calf's leg, leans into the picture, and is overlapped by the powerful, striding figure of a follower entwined in snakes.

BACCHUS AND ARIADNE
Titian; 1520–23; 175.2 x 190.5 cm (69 x 75 in); oil on canvas
This is one of three mythological paintings completed by Titian for Alfonso d'Este's *Camerino d'Alabastro* (Italian: "Alabaster Chamber") in his castle at Ferrara, in Italy. Raphael (p. 48) was originally commissioned to paint the story of Bacchus and Ariadne, but on his death the commission passed to Titian. The painting is based on tales told by the Roman poets Ovid and Catullus, and shows the wine god Bacchus coming to the aid of Ariadne, the daughter of King Minos. She had been abandoned by her lover, Theseus, on the island of Naxos. Elements of the story are represented throughout the painting (left; above right), while the composition focuses on the figure of Bacchus. The unbridled energy of his pose (he is positioned in mid-air) is set off by the brilliance of the colouring and the expansive landscape. Bacchus is followed by his carousing retinue – some of their poses are borrowed from classical statues; the figure with snakes is based on the *Laocoön* (p. 50).

NARRATIVE DETAIL
The departing ship of Theseus is shown on the sea in the distance.

ORIGINS OF THE MILKY WAY
Tintoretto; c.1578; 148 x 165.1 cm (58¼ x 65 in); oil on canvas
Titian's paintings created a vogue for mythological subjects in Venice in the 16th century. Tintoretto (1518–94) was greatly indebted to him, but he was also critical of the older master's methods, writing his own formula for success on the wall of his room: "The drawing of Michelangelo and the colouring of Titian". This mythological picture, like the religious works that Tintoretto painted, shows off his energetic draughtsmanship and his love of dramatic light effects.

PORTRAIT OF A MAN
Titian; c.1511; 81.2 x 66.3 cm (32 x 26 in); oil on canvas
Titian excelled as a portraitist, immortalizing the features of many of the most powerful men in Europe: he painted magnificent portraits of the Emperor Charles V; Francis I, the King of France; and Philip II of Spain. This early work may be a self-portrait, and it is a supremely confident demonstration of Titian's artistic powers. One of the most impressive features is the luxurious blue silk sleeve, which is bathed in light and seems to drape over the illusionistic stone parapet, out of the picture space. Another is the calm, self-assured gaze of the sitter, which unwaveringly meets our own.

The High Renaissance

THE YEAR 1500 MARKS a subtle shift in artistic style and objectives. The new phase, which is popularly known as the High Renaissance, is usually associated with the careers of the Italian giants, Michelangelo, Raphael, and Titian. To Vasari, writing in 1550, the key to the new artistic style was *"grazia"*, meaning a refined grace and ease of manner. Even the most contrived details were made to appear effortless and unforced. In technical terms, oil was the ideal medium for displaying this *grazia* – colours could be blended to create effects of softness and charm. It was perfect, too, for expressing the "boldness" of each artist's personal style, which had become so highly valued. Individuality was also measured by the artist's inventiveness and the scope of his imaginative powers: no challenge was too great, no pose too complex, no scale too grand!

PORTRAIT OF BALDASSARE CASTIGLIONE
Raphael; c.1514–15; 82 x 66 cm (32¼ x 26 in); oil on canvas
The great Raphael (1483–1520) painted this portrait of his friend, Castiglione, who wrote the *Book of the Courtier* (1528; below). Like many High Renaissance portraits, it is painstakingly designed to look both simple and sophisticated. The count displays the inner calm required of a gentleman.

THE ART OF THE COURTIER
Castiglione's influential treatise, which describes an ideal of courtly behaviour at the Italian ducal court of Urbino (below), expresses the idea that art should conceal the work that goes into its creation. The artist, like the courtier, was to appear effortlessly accomplished in all fields.

The Ducal Palace of Urbino

Urbino enjoyed fame as a cultural centre under the Montefeltro dukes

THE APOLLO BELVEDERE
The elegant pose of this Roman statue provided artists with a model of grace, ease, and power in movement. Dating from the 2nd century A.D., the statue is a marble copy of an ancient Greek bronze. It was found in the late 15th century and became the pride of Pope Julius II's new Belvedere Collection of sculpture (p. 58).

The delicately joined hands are based on life studies

THE ARCHANGEL RAPHAEL WITH TOBIAS
Pietro Perugino; c.1500–5; 113.3 x 56.5 cm (44½ x 22¼ in); oil and tempera on panel
The Umbrian Perugino (c.1450–1523) was one of the most successful Italian painters in the 1480s and 1490s. The charm and sweetness of his figures were imitated by his young assistant, Raphael, who was to combine these qualities with Leonardo's new, grand Florentine style (pp. 36–37). Perugino was praised for his graceful method of colouring in oils, which he had mastered by studying Flemish examples (pp. 20–21). In this panel, which is part of an altarpiece, Perugino's skill in the painting of light effects can be seen in the luminous reflections of the flesh, the fish's scales, and the boy's lustrous hair (detail, left). Tobias is artfully posed in the classical manner – with his body curving to take the weight on one leg – but a preparatory drawing shows that both figures were drawn from life: a boy and an assistant had posed.

THE GARVAGH MADONNA

Raphael; c.1508–10; 38.7 x 32.7 cm (15¼ x 13 in); oil on panel

Raphael's paintings of the Virgin and Child present an image of idealized nature. Following the practice of the time, Raphael has selected the most beautiful elements from nature (drawing from life), and combined them with the best details and ideas from works by other masters: for example, the pyramidical figure composition is borrowed from Leonardo. The gesture of the Virgin holding her drapery comes from Roman sculpture – senators were shown holding their togas in a similar way.

THE BATTLE OF ISSUS

Albrecht Altdorfer; 1529; 158.4 x 120.3 cm (62½ x 47½ in); oil on panel

With growing confidence, artists extended their range of subject-matter, even attempting to capture the dazzling atmospheric effects of nature and portraying its infinite grandeur. While Italian painters represented landscapes, clouds, night skies, and the shimmering sun as part of the human environment, the German artist Albrecht Altdorfer (c.1480–1538) presented humanity as a tiny "speck" in the vast eternal scheme of things, its struggles and strivings dwarfed by the cosmic forces of nature.

This spectacular battle scene, with its fantastic, seething sky (detail, below right), is more astonishing for being represented on a relatively small scale. In his bird's-eye view of the scene, Altdorfer has transcended the limitations of his panel to convey the world's true magnitude.

The glory of the setting sun evokes the splendour of nature

ASSUMPTION OF THE VIRGIN

Correggio; 1526–30; 10.93 x 11.95 m (35 ft 10 in x 39 ft 2 in); fresco

While Altdorfer's modestly sized panel provided no obstacle to his grand vision, many artists realized that largeness of scale could only add to the impact of their works. The High Renaissance saw the creation of numerous works on a daringly colossal scale, from Michelangelo's *David* (p. 54), to the architecture of the new St. Peter's (p. 51), and Correggio's great illusionistic dome paintings in Parma Cathedral (left). Illusionism – where the painter uses perspective tricks to give the illusion of an alternative reality – presented one of the most obvious opportunities for artists to display their skill. The northern Italian painter Correggio (c.1494–1534), who learned many of his tricks from Mantegna, surpassed him in boldness and ingenuity, solving every problem with stylish ease. The effect is miraculous: the eye spirals upwards from the Apostles on the dome's lower rim, through angels and cloud-borne cherubim, to the Virgin in the heavens.

The windows flood the interior of the dome with light, adding to its visionary impact

Rome's renewal

RECONSTRUCTING ANCIENT ROME
The antiquarian Marco Fabio Calvo collaborated with Raphael in his scientific reconstruction of ancient Rome's appearance. This woodcut, from Calvo's book of 1527, shows the main surviving monuments presented in a circular plan.

When Raphael arrived in Rome in 1508, Pope Julius II had already embarked on his ambitious plans to restore the ailing city to its ancient grandeur. Rome had only become the continual residence of the Papacy under Pope Nicholas V (1447–55), when alterations were begun. Now cardinals and wealthy individuals, encouraged by major tax concessions on property, busily erected splendid palaces, churches, and buildings – while Roman remains were unearthed during construction work. The Sienese banker Agostino Chigi, a financier to the popes, built the "Villa Farnesina"; even its stable block, designed by the young Raphael, was calculated to be grander than a palace. The major architectural project of the period was the building of the new St. Peter's, which consumed the talents of its first architect, Donato Bramante (c.1444–1514), and others, including Michelangelo and Raphael. It devoured marble from Rome's ancient ruins, although Leo X (Julius II's successor) had put Raphael in charge of preserving Rome's archaeological heritage. The flurry of artistic activity was abruptly interrupted by the Sack of Rome in 1527, when French troops ravaged the city, forcing its artists and citizens to flee.

LAOCOON
2nd–1st century B.C.; height: 2.45 m (8 ft); marble
The exciting discovery in a vineyard on the Esquiline Hill, on 14 January 1506, of the antique sculpture known as the *Laocoön* had a huge impact on artists in Rome. Michelangelo and the architect Giuliano da Sangallo saw it when it was still in the ground, and recognized it as the ancient Greek group described by Pliny as "a work to be preferred to all that the arts of painting and sculpture have produced".

The group shows the Trojan priest Laocoön and his sons being crushed to death by snakes

THE TRIUMPH OF GALATEA
Raphael; 1511; 295 x 225 cm (116 x 88½ in); fresco
The airy garden rooms of Chigi's Villa Farnesina (below) were used for lavish entertaining. They were decorated with mythological scenes in the manner of ancient imperial Rome: Raphael's famous fresco of *Galatea* complements scenes in the same *"loggia"* (an external gallery) by other artists, including the Sienese architect and painter Baldassare Peruzzi (1481–1536). Peruzzi painted Chigi's horoscope on the ceiling vault, as well as designing the villa itself. The source for Raphael's fresco was "Verses for the Joust of Giuliano de' Medici" by Politian (p. 33), in which he describes an engraved image of the sea nymph Galatea – riding on a shell pulled by dolphins and accompanied by sea creatures and *"amorini"* (little "Cupids") – which appears on the doors of the Palace of Venus. It seems that Raphael was emulating the beauty of a lost masterpiece.

THE VILLA FARNESINA
The Villa Farnesina (1508–11) was designed by Peruzzi in the classical style of a Roman country house, with two projecting wings. He also painted the false perspective views of the *Salone delle Prospettive* inside. Peruzzi's elegant style led to his appointment as a co-architect of St. Peter's (above right) on Raphael's death in 1520.

BRAMANTE'S PLANS

Bramante's plan of 1506 (left) and Caradosso's bronze medal (right), which was struck to commemorate the design for the exterior, give us some idea of the scale of the architect's ambitions for the new St. Peter's. The church was planned in the shape of a Greek cross (having four equal "arms"), with a tall turret at each outer corner. It was to be crowned by a massive dome on the huge scale of Rome's ancient Pantheon.

This shows Bramante's original design: note the differences to the finished version (below)

The new St. Peter's

The old Basilica of St. Peter's stood over the alleged grave of St. Peter, a shrine for all Christendom. It was erected in A.D. 324 by Constantine the Great and survived in dilapidated form until Julius II's reign, when it was pulled down to make way for a church of unsurpassed splendour. The foundation stone for the new St. Peter's was laid in 1506, and its design entrusted to the esteemed, but elderly, architect Bramante. It was to occupy ten architects before its final completion, over 120 years later.

The completed dome was much higher than the shallow dome planned

MICHELANGELO'S CONTRIBUTION

Bramante constructed the piers (large supporting pillars) and arches to the dome, but the building did not begin to take its present form (right) until 1546, when Michelangelo was made architect by Pope Paul III. He worked on it until his death in 1564, designing the back of the church and the dome (completed by Giacomo della Porta in 1593).

The dome's jutting rim and plain niches on the drum make it look like a piece of solid sculpture

Bramante adopted the circular form of ancient temples instead of the square crucifix form of Renaissance churches

A RENAISSANCE TEMPLE

Bramante's *Tempietto* (Italian: "Little Temple") at San Pietro in Montorio, Rome (1502), is considered to be the embodiment of High Renaissance architecture. It marks the spot where St. Peter was believed to have been crucified, and looks more like a sculptural monument than a building. Perfectly round and unadorned by ornament, it has the austere, monumental dignity of a full-size classical temple: artists of the High Renaissance tried to recreate both the style and spirit of ancient Rome.

DECORATIVE SCHEMES

The fresco decoration of Cardinal Bibbiena's Vatican *loggia*, completed in 1516 by Raphael and his chief assistant, Giovanni da Udine, was inspired by decorative paintings found in the subterranean rooms of the Golden House of Nero and in a Roman ruin near the Church of San Pietro in Vincoli. Their light, graceful ornamental forms – a mixture of plants, human figures, and fantastic creatures – were called "grotesques", from *grotte* (Italian: "caves").

Raphael's Vatican rooms

RAPHAEL'S FAST-GROWING reputation in Florence brought him to the attention of Pope Julius II in Rome. By 1509 he was hard at work on a suite of papal apartments – his three *stanze* ("rooms") – in Rome's magnificent Vatican palace, while Michelangelo laboured under lock and key on the Vatican's Sistine Chapel Ceiling nearby (pp. 56–57). The first room Raphael completed, the so-called *Stanza della Segnatura* ("Room of the Signature") established his reputation immediately. Its frescoes, with their graceful classical poses and grand compositions, have been copied by countless artists over the centuries. Raphael created a vigorous dramatic style in the second room, the *Stanza d'Eliodoro* ("Room of Heliodorus"). The aged Pope died before its completion, and the final *Stanza dell'Incendio* ("Room of the Fire") was painted, with the help of pupils, under Pope Leo X.

PHILOSOPHY
Raphael depicted the themes of the *Stanza della Segnatura* in four medallions on the ceiling – female figures represent Philosophy (above), Theology, Poetry, and Jurisprudence. Under each is the fresco that brings its learned discipline to life; the ancient thinkers (below) appear under *Philosophy* (above).

The School of Athens

RAPHAEL *c.1510–12; lunette: 7.72 m (25 ft 4 in) at base; fresco*
The *Stanza della Segnatura* was probably intended to be Pope Julius II's private library. Appropriately, the ceiling shows the four disciplines (above right) under which books would have been classified, while the wall frescoes depict all the literary heroes of classical and Christian times: the ancient philosophers of *The School of Athens* (right) appear on the wall opposite learned theologians, discussing the mystery of the Sacrament; and the great poets of *Parnassus* (far right) face the lawmakers.
The famous *School of Athens* was painted in about 1510–12, at a time when the first section of Michelangelo's ceiling was unveiled (14 August 1511) – the bulky figure resting on a block in the foreground, which is not in the preparatory cartoon, seems to imitate Michelangelo's prophets and sibyls (pp. 56–57).

LOGICAL POSITIONS
The careful placing of numerous figures within a deep perspective setting looks back to the methods of Ghiberti (p. 14). Raphael has extended similar precision to the poses of each individual figure. Every gesture and movement (based on classical sculpture) is as logically determined as the mathematical perspective construction.

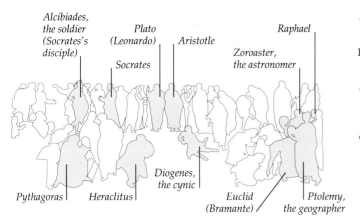

Alcibiades, the soldier (Socrates's disciple) | Plato (Leonardo) | Aristotle | Raphael

Socrates | Zoroaster, the astronomer

Pythagoras | Heraclitus | Diogenes, the cynic | Euclid (Bramante) | Ptolemy, the geographer

ANCIENT PHILOSOPHERS

Various figures have been identified in *The School of Athens*. In the centre are the Greek philosophers, Plato (modelled on Leonardo) and Aristotle. Their gestures – Plato points to the heavens, while Aristotle extends his hand towards earthbound reality – indicate the sources of their ideas. Raphael has even included himself among the pupils.

POPE JULIUS II

Raphael; c.1511–12; 108 x 80. 7 cm (42½ x 31¼ in); oil on panel

During his reign, Pope Julius II (1503–1513) set Rome at the very centre of Italy's cultural achievements. He not only commissioned Michelangelo's Sistine Ceiling and Raphael's *stanze*, but also founded the famous Belvedere Collection of sculpture (p. 58) and began the new St. Peter's (p. 51). In the political sphere, he was a brilliant financial reformer, an astute diplomat, and a skilful military campaigner. Raphael's fine portrait shows the Pope in the year before his death. His chairback is topped with acorns, from the oak emblem of the della Rovere family, to which he belonged. (These acorns also appear on the Sistine Ceiling.)

THE LIBERATION OF ST. PETER FROM PRISON

Raphael; c.1512–13; lunette: 6.60 m (21 ft 8 in) at base; fresco

The *Stanza d'Eliodoro* – named after one of its frescoes, the *Expulsion of Heliodorus* – shows miraculous events in the history of the Christian Church. The most remarkable scene is the *Liberation of St. Peter*, which is painted around a window, making the fresco appear even darker. As St. Peter sleeps in his cell, an angel appears in a blaze of light, causing the chains to fall from his hands. The saint is led out (on the right), while the soldiers (on the left) stumble, dazzled by the radiance. The episode was particularly relevant, for Pope Julius II's troops had recently liberated Italy from the French, and he had given thanks in the Church of San Pietro in Vincoli ("St. Peter in Chains").

COPYING RAPHAEL

During Raphael's lifetime, the fame of his compositions was spread by the engraver Marcantonio Raimondi of Bologna (c.1480–1534), who offered his services to Raphael in Rome. This engraving shows the *Parnassus* fresco of Apollo, muses, and poets in the *Stanza della Segnatura*, and was made after a finished drawing that differs in details from the fresco.

Michelangelo's "divine" powers

THE FLORENTINE SCULPTOR, painter, poet, and architect Michelangelo Buonarroti (1475–1564) pushed the artistic ideals of his generation to their physical and stylistic extremes. Born into minor nobility, he learned fresco techniques in the workshop of Ghirlandaio (p. 13), and trained as a sculptor. In his youth, he copied frescoes by Giotto and Masaccio, and studied Donatello's sculpture. Inspired by their heroic example, and that of antique sculpture, he developed an ideal based on the physical expressiveness of the male nude. The grace and awe-inspiring scale of his works had a huge impact: Michelangelo unwittingly fostered the cult of the genius with superhuman powers, transforming the way artists regarded themselves and their works.

MICHELANGELO
This bust of Michelangelo appears on his tomb in Santa Croce, Florence, which was designed by Giorgio Vasari. It is to Vasari that we owe the idea of Michelangelo as the artist "who surpasses them all".

David's sling is barely visible: his strength derives from his moral courage

The hands, the most expressive elements, are shown exceptionally large

DAVID
Michelangelo; 1501–4; height: 4.09 m (13 ft 5 in); marble
Michelangelo's *David* is the largest free-standing marble statue since classical times. The shepherd boy who defeated the giant Goliath is transformed into an ancient hero of unrivalled grace and beauty. His powerful body is both indolently sensual and athletic, the head (detail, left) is noble and idealized. Michelangelo's mastery of anatomy is seen in every muscle and sinew; he even details the bulging veins in the hands. Towering over the people at the entrance to the Palazzo Vecchio, *David* stood as a symbol of Florence's supremacy.

*"My beard toward Heaven, I feel the back
of my brain,
Upon my nape I grow the breast
of a Harpy;
My brush, above my face continually,
Makes it a splendid floor by dripping down."*

Michelangelo, Sonnet 64, verse 2

THE CARRARA MARBLE QUARRIES
The dimensions of *David* were dictated by a massive shallow block of marble, quarried in 1466, in which a figure of a giant had been blocked out, botched, and then abandoned. Michelangelo rose to the challenge. For the *Julius Tomb* (opposite), however, he spent eight months at the Italian marble quarries of Carrara, selecting suitable blocks.

MICHELANGELO'S POETRY
Michelangelo was one of the greatest poets of his age. His sonnets poignantly, and sometimes humorously, express his spiritual and artistic struggles. The sonnet above, written in 1511, lightheartedly relates the very real physical torments of painting the Sistine Chapel Ceiling (pp. 56–57).

THE DONI TONDO
Michelangelo; c.1506–8; diameter: 120 cm (47¼ in); tempera on panel
The *Doni Tondo*, the only completed panel painting by Michelangelo to survive, was commissioned by Angelo Doni to mark his marriage to Maddalena Strozzi. The complex, interlocking poses of the Holy Family were based on a cartoon by Leonardo and were designed to echo the curves of the *tondo* (Italian: "round painting"). The artfully posed male nudes in the background may have been included to show Michelangelo's skill in this field.

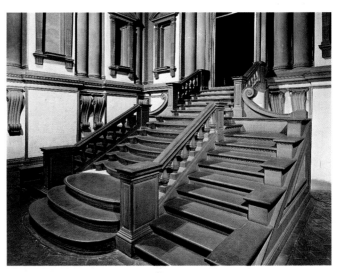

THE LAURENTIAN LIBRARY STAIRCASE
Michelangelo's design for the architectural framework of the *Julius Tomb* led to a lifelong fascination with architecture. For the Medici, he built the New Sacristy of San Lorenzo in Florence and began work on the Laurentian Library next door. Its staircase (above) was later executed to one of Michelangelo's designs, and shows how he has begun to use forms expressively, freeing them from their structural purpose. Michelangelo's most important commission was the completion of the new St. Peter's, which was largely realized in his lifetime.

Moses's horns come from the common misinterpretation of a Biblical passage describing light radiating from his head

Moses has the *terribilità* (Italian: "awesome power") so admired by Michelangelo's contemporaries

THE TRAGEDY OF THE JULIUS TOMB
In 1505, Pope Julius II summoned Michelangelo to Rome to create a magnificent free-standing tomb for him, on the scale of the famous mausoleums of antiquity. Fired with enthusiasm for the scheme, which was destined to take pride of place in the old St. Peter's, Michelangelo hastened to Carrara to select the marble for 40 figures, which were to be more than life-size. The Pope's interest in the project soon evaporated (probably due to the plan to build a new St. Peter's). Julius II died in 1513, and the ill-fated project staggered to completion in 1545. It had dwindled to the shrunken tomb (above) that now stands in San Pietro in Vincoli in Rome. Only *Moses* (c.1515; right) and the niches (1506) are by Michelangelo's hand.

THE CROSSED-LEG CAPTIVE
Michelangelo; 1527–28; height: 2.77 m (9 ft 1 in); marble
This unfinished slave, intended for the *Julius Tomb*, reveals Michelangelo's method of sculpting by cutting into the front of the block, rather than from all sides. To the artist it seemed that he was freeing the emerging figure – the embodiment of his idea – from its prison of stone.

The Sistine Ceiling

MICHELANGELO'S SISTINE CHAPEL Ceiling in the Vatican represents the summit of his achievement. It was commissioned by Pope Julius II in 1508, partly to make amends for abandoning the project of the *Julius Tomb* (p. 55). Many of the titanic figures intended for the tomb seem to have been included on the ceiling vault. The Pope originally wanted Michelangelo to depict the twelve Apostles and cover the old, blue, star-spangled ceiling with a fashionable, ornamental scheme. But Michelangelo declared that this would be "a poor thing", and a more spectacular, erudite plan was devised. Majestic Old Testament prophets and ancient sibyls (female seers) now flanked the main vault, which was painted with the epic story of Noah and the Creation.

THE BELVEDERE TORSO
The twisted poses of the *"ignudi"* – idealized nudes at the corners of the main scenes – were based on this torso (c.50 A.D.).

THE DELPHIC SIBYL
Michelangelo; 1509; 350 x 380 cm (137¾ x 149½ in); fresco
The classical sibyls, who uttered prophecies and oracles, were named after their places of origin: the young Delphic Sibyl is associated with the Greek oracle at Delphi. Surviving drawings show that Michelangelo's sibyls were based on muscular male models. This image, from the blackened ceiling before it was cleaned, shows the "stony" colouring that deceived viewers into thinking the figures were painted to resemble marble sculpture.

COLOUR INSPIRATION
Michelangelo is seen as the creator of the "artificial" Mannerist (pp. 60–61) style of colouring. He inspired the early Mannerist master Pontormo (p. 61) to use vivid hues of unearthly delicacy.

The pale colours of the Virgin's robes accentuate the figure's spirituality

Detail of Pontormo's *Annunciation* from the Capponi Chapel in Santa Felicità, Florence

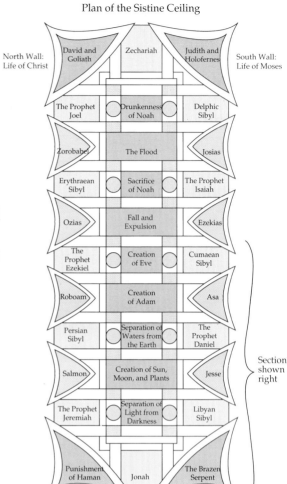

Plan of the Sistine Ceiling

North Wall: Life of Christ

South Wall: Life of Moses

David and Goliath	Zechariah	Judith and Holofernes
The Prophet Joel	Drunkenness of Noah	Delphic Sibyl
Zorobabel	The Flood	Josias
Erythraean Sibyl	Sacrifice of Noah	The Prophet Isaiah
Ozias	Fall and Expulsion	Ezekias
The Prophet Ezekiel	Creation of Eve	Cumaean Sibyl
Roboam	Creation of Adam	Asa
Persian Sibyl	Separation of Waters from the Earth	The Prophet Daniel
Salmon	Creation of Sun, Moon, and Plants	Jesse
The Prophet Jeremiah	Separation of Light from Darkness	Libyan Sibyl
Punishment of Haman	Jonah	The Brazen Serpent

Section shown right

West Wall; Altar; Michelangelo's *Last Judgement* (1535–41)

Colour Key:

Central panels: the story of Noah and the Creation

Prophets and sibyls

Ignudi

Corner spandrels: Old Testament scenes

Vaulting compartments: ancestors of Christ

Simulated bronze medallions

THE MEANING OF THE CEILING
The overall theme of the ceiling has been much discussed. It is now thought that the episodes from the Old Testament and the sayings of the prophets and sibyls are linked because, according to a medieval tradition, they foretell the coming of Christ. For this reason, Christ's ancestors are shown. The scheme was designed to complement earlier wall paintings of the lives of Moses and Christ by other artists.

MICHELANGELO'S TRUE COLOURS
This shows the *Delphic Sibyl* after cleaning, and vividly displays the loveliness and originality of Michelangelo's colouring. The draperies are painted in radiant contrasting hues, which imitate the colour shifts of shot silk. Such *cangiante* (Italian: "changing") colouring had previously been reserved largely for the robes and wings of angels. Michelangelo, however, uses it for the entire ceiling, endowing his figures with grace and vitality. He had intended to enrich the colouristic effect by retouching areas in ultramarine blue and gold, but the Pope's impatience to see the ceiling completed meant such details had to be sacrificed.

The Sistine Ceiling (section)

MICHELANGELO *1508–12; 13 x 36 m (42 ft 8 in x 118 ft); fresco*

Michelangelo made over two hundred preliminary drawings for the ceiling, which were painstakingly made into cartoons. These full-size working designs were laid against the wet plaster, which was applied to the ceiling each day, and the outlines were traced with a stylus (grooves can still be seen). Michelangelo frescoed the huge vault alone, having dismissed his helpers because their work was so inferior. He painted from a standing position in great discomfort, and refused to admit anyone into the chapel as he laboured. Work was often interrupted; early sections became mouldy – pigments reacted with the plaster – and he ran out of funds. In 1512, after four and a half years of intolerable exertion, the ceiling was finally unveiled. The artist's vision of God's power and humanity's spiritual awakening left everyone speechless with admiration.

The North and Italy

FOLLOWING DÜRER'S EXAMPLE (pp. 40–41), Northern artists of the early 16th century began to study and absorb the ideas of the Italian Renaissance. In Augsburg, the wealthy commercial centre of Germany, painters like Hans Holbein the Younger (p. 43) sought inspiration from northern Italy. Antwerp, with its busy port and resident foreign merchants, evolved an eclectic style that was to dominate 16th-century Northern art, in which Flemish and Italian elements were fused. The "Romanists", Jan Gossaert (c.1478–1532) and Jan van Scorel (1495–1562), looked directly to the antique and to its Italian intermediaries like Leonardo, Raphael, and Michelangelo. Gossaert was the first Northern artist to study Roman antiques through the support of a patron, while Van Scorel succeeded Raphael as the curator of the Belvedere Collection of antiquities in the Vatican.

ROME'S BELVEDERE COLLECTION
The Romanists regarded the ancient past as an idyllic era. Gossaert's interests coincided with those of his patron, Philip of Burgundy, who took the artist with him on his diplomatic mission to the Vatican in about 1508. There, Gossaert made a record of the classical sculpture in the Belvedere Collection. This collection had been formed in 1503 by Pope Julius II, who had begun to place the newly excavated classical works of art in the Belvedere Court (shown in this engraving). By the time Van Scorel was put in charge of the collection in 1522, it included treasures like this Roman sculpture of *Venus Felix and Amor* (right), placed there in 1509.

Like Italian artists, Gossaert and Van Scorel were influenced by the idealized forms of antique sculpture

NEPTUNE AND AMPHITRITE
Jan Gossaert; 1516; 188 x 123.8 cm (74 x 48¾ in); oil on panel
In 1515, Gossaert began a series of mythological paintings for Philip of Burgundy's castle, working with the Venetian printmaker and painter Jacopo de' Barbari (c.1440–1516). Barbari died just as work began, and Gossaert took over, creating in his *Neptune and Amphitrite* the first nudes of Flemish painting to be genuinely classically inspired. The poses are taken from Barbari's well-known print of *Mars and Venus* (below), but Gossaert has made the forms heavier and more sensuous. The monumentality of the figures is enhanced by the illusionistic ancient architecture that they so solidly inhabit.

MARS AND VENUS
Jacopo de' Barbari was a significant figure in the blending of Northern and Italian styles. He made his name in northern Europe, working at the courts of Emperor Maximilian and Frederick the Wise of Saxony in Germany, and for Margaret of Austria and Philip of Burgundy in the Netherlands. His mythological prints helped to spread the concept of the Italian nude in the North and profoundly influenced Dürer, who used them in his own studies of the human nude (p. 30).

A GROTESQUE OLD WOMAN
After Quinten Massys; 1510/20;
64.1 x 45.4 cm (25¼ x 18 in); oil on panel
Antwerp's leading painter, Quinten
Massys (c.1465–1530), was a veritable
"magpie" in his borrowings from
different artistic styles. This portrait
(made famous in the 19th century,
when it was used to illustrate the
Duchess in Lewis Carroll's *Alice's
Adventures in Wonderland*) was
inspired by Leonardo's caricatures.

BONIFACIUS AMERBACH
Hans Holbein the Younger; 1519; 28.5 x
27.5 cm (11¼ x 11 in); tempera on panel
This portrait by Holbein seems
naturalistic, but is actually carefully
contrived. Painted on his return
from northern Italy, it has certain
Venetian characteristics, such as the
atmospheric contrasts of light and
shade. However, Venetian portraits
of this period were themselves
indebted to Northern examples.

THE PRESENTATION OF CHRIST IN THE TEMPLE
Jan van Scorel; c.1530–35; 114 x 85 cm
(45 x 33½ in); oil on panel
Van Scorel's refined blending of Italian and Northern
elements has earned him the nickname of the "Northern
Raphael". He experienced Italian art at first hand, visiting
Venice in about 1519, and taking up residence in Rome
from 1522 for his prestigious Vatican appointment under
Pope Adrian IV, a fellow Dutchman. This picture shows
how thoroughly he had studied the art and architecture
of Rome. The temple is in the style of Bramante (p. 51),
and the proportions and draperies of the figures reveal
an awareness of Italian style. However, the naturalistic
relationship between the figures and the airy space they
occupy, as well as the emphasis on the architecture
itself, is more Northern than Italian.

AN ELDERLY COUPLE
Jan Gossaert; c.1520–25; 45.7 x 67.3 cm
(18 x 26½ in); oil on vellum
This double portrait of an elderly
man and his wife draws on a long
tradition of Flemish portraiture,
where penetrating observation of an
individual (often close to caricature)
is combined with monumentality.
Half-length double portraits, in
which the sitters' differences are
subtly emphasized, were popular in
Italy, Germany, and the Netherlands
from the mid-15th century. Here, the
raised and lowered gazes suggest
active and passive personalities.

Mannerism

The label "Mannerism" – from the Italian *maniera*, meaning "style" – is often applied to art in the period from about 1520 to 1580. Mannerist works are refined, sophisticated, and technically accomplished: they are deliberately stylish, making a cult of the beautiful and delighting in bizarre, fanciful imagery. However, there is a problem with the Mannerist label, in that it has come to symbolize an abrupt break with the ideals of the High Renaissance. Mannerist art has been seen as decadent and neurotic, at odds with the ideals of harmony and grace established by preceding generations. Now, modern definitions of Mannerism regard it as more of a continuation and elaboration of trends set in motion by the High Renaissance. It draws on, for example, the suave grace and theatricality of Raphael's mature compositions, as well as Michelangelo's skill in portraying the male nude, from the taut muscular forms and artful poses to his stylized borrowings from the antique (a constant source of inspiration).

SELF-PORTRAIT IN A CONVEX MIRROR
Parmigianino; 1524;
diameter: 24.3 cm (9½ in); oil on panel
This self-portrait, by the Italian Parmigianino (1503–40), is a self-consciously clever image. It is both natural and contrived, faithfully reproducing the mirror's strange distortions.

THE BATTLE OF CASCINA
Aristotile da Sangallo; 1542; 76.2 x 132 cm (30 x 52 in); grisaille on panel
Michelangelo was the artist most admired by the Mannerists – this is a copy of his famous lost cartoon of *The Battle of Cascina*. Michelangelo's cartoon, made in competition with Leonardo's *Battle of Anghiari* for the decoration of the Grand Council Chamber in Florence, shows the bathing soldiers startled by the call to battle, an ideal subject to show off his mastery of the nude. It is a storehouse of idealized and tortuously complex poses – all of which demonstrate astonishing accomplishment.

TWISTING MOVEMENT
This detail shows the ostentatious and deliberate difficulty of the poses that Michelangelo set himself.

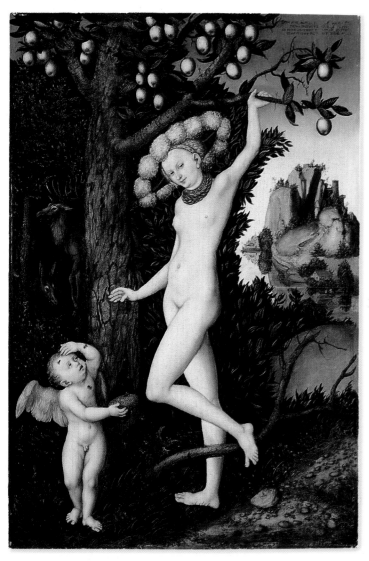

CUPID COMPLAINING TO VENUS
Lucas Cranach the Elder; 1530; 81.3 x 54.6 cm (32 x 21½ in); oil on panel
In the North, Cranach developed a refined style that has parallels with Italian Mannerism. Like his Italian colleagues, Cranach was influenced by prevailing aristocratic tastes: in 1505, he succeeded Jacopo de' Barbari as court painter to Frederick the Wise, and worked in an atmosphere of relaxed elegance and sophisticated pleasures. *Cupid Complaining to Venus* exudes a mannered grace and sensuality: the eyes even have a feline quality. His Venus, however, is portrayed as a fashionable beauty, complete with hat and jewellery, rather than an idealized Italianate nude.

An Allegory with Venus and Cupid

AGNOLO BRONZINO *1540–45; 146.1 x 116.2 cm
(57½ x 45¾ in); oil on panel*

This sophisticated image by the great Mannerist Agnolo Bronzino (1503–72) symbolizes erotic passion. Stylistically, it is indebted to Michelangelo and his *Doni Tondo* (p. 55), but Bronzino has exchanged the physical and emotional intensity of the Holy Family for a languid sensuality and cool detachment. Venus and her incestuous lover Cupid are shown with idealized and elongated bodies, unaware of the destructive nature of their love. The half-girl/half-beast offering a honeycomb shows how love's sweetness also has a sting in its tail.

BIZARRE CREATIONS
This shows a fantastic mask of Venus by Giovanni Battista Rosso (1495–1540), designed for one of King Francis I's elaborate pageants at Fontainebleau, in France. It exhibits the Mannerist taste for bizarre ornament.

UNSEEING FACES
The masks, with their vacant eyes, symbolize deceit (detail, above), and also emphasize the atmosphere of artificiality.

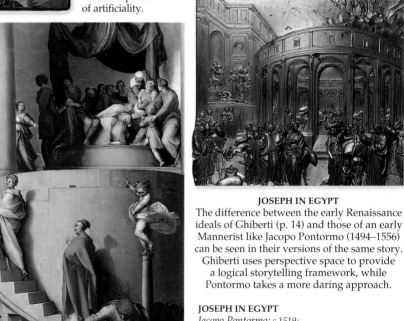

JOSEPH IN EGYPT
The difference between the early Renaissance ideals of Ghiberti (p. 14) and those of an early Mannerist like Jacopo Pontormo (1494–1556) can be seen in their versions of the same story. Ghiberti uses perspective space to provide a logical storytelling framework, while Pontormo takes a more daring approach.

JOSEPH IN EGYPT
*Jacopo Pontormo; c.1519;
96.5 x 109.5 cm (38 x 43 in); oil on panel*
Pontormo's picture reveals how radically artistic objectives had changed over the Renaissance period. Ghiberti's narrative is clear, his composition harmonious, and the space is carefully arranged. In Pontormo's scene, the staircase flamboyantly sweeps nowhere, the figures are grouped here and there, and the different episodes of the story are difficult to isolate. The emphasis is on pattern and fantastic invention, in keeping with the decorative nature of the work.

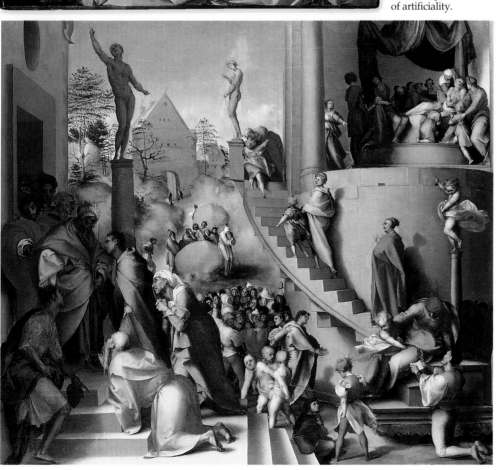

Chronology

1266/67 Birth of Giotto.

1302 Papal Bull proclaiming papal supremacy over national rulers.

1302–10 Giovanni Pisano working on Pisa Cathedral pulpit.

1304 Birth of Petrarch.

1308 Dante begins his *Divine Comedy*.

1309 Papacy moves from Rome to Avignon because of unrest.

c.1305 Giotto paints Arena Chapel.

1311 Duccio's *Maestà* carried in procession to Siena Cathedral.

1317 Venetian fleet makes longest sea voyage to date.

1319 Death of Duccio.

1321 Death of Dante.

1337 Death of Giotto.
Beginning of Hundred Years War between France and England.

1338 Ambrogio Lorenzetti paints *Good Government* frescoes, Palazzo Pubblico, Siena.

c.1339 Birth of Rogier van der Weyden.

1340 Simone Martini working at papal court in Avignon.

1344 Death of Simone Martini.

1348 The Great Plague devastates Europe; probably claims life of Ambrogio Lorenzetti.

1353 Publication of Boccaccio's *Decameron*.

1364 Charles V becomes King of France.

c.1370 Birth of Gentile da Fabriano.

1374 Death of Petrarch.

1375 Death of Boccaccio.

1376 Return of Papacy to Rome.

1377 Birth of Brunelleschi.
Richard II becomes King of England.

1378 Birth of Ghiberti.
Rival line of popes elected; Western Church divided.

c.1386 Birth of Donatello.

1397 Birth of Uccello.

1400 Birth of Luca della Robbia.
High point of International Gothic style.

1401 Birth of Masaccio.

1405/6 Death of Claus Sluter.

c.1406 Birth of Fra Filippo Lippi.

c.1415/20 Birth of Piero della Francesca.

1416 Limbourg Brothers decorate *Les Très Riches Heures du Duc de Berry*.

1419 Philip the Good becomes Duke of Burgundy.

1420 Brunelleschi begins work on the dome of Florence Cathedral.

1424 Masaccio and Masolino begin the Brancacci Chapel frescoes.

1427 Death of Gentile da Fabriano.

c.1428 Death of Masaccio.

1431 Birth of Mantegna.

1434 Medici family become dominant faction in Florence.
Van Eyck paints *The Arnolfini Marriage*.

1435 Birth of Verrocchio.
Birth of Giovanni Bellini.
Alberti completes *On Painting*.

1441 Death of Van Eyck.

1444 Birth of Bramante.

1445 Donatello begins *Gattamelata*.
Birth of Botticelli.

1446 Death of Brunelleschi.

1447 Death of Masolino.
Nicholas V becomes Pope.

1449 Birth of Ghirlandaio.

c.1450 Rogier van der Weyden's probable trip to Italy.
Gutenberg's invention of printing using movable type.

1452 Birth of Leonardo.
Ghiberti completes Baptistery doors.

1453 Hundred Years War ends.
Turks capture Constantinople; the end of the Byzantine Empire.

1455 Death of Ghiberti.
Death of Fra Angelico.
Wars of the Roses begins in England.

1457 Death of Andrea del Castagno.

1460 Birth of Grünewald.
Birth of Antonio del Pollaiuolo.

1464 Death of Van der Weyden.

c.1465 Birth of Quinten Massys.

1466 Death of Donatello.

1467 Charles the Bold becomes Duke of Burgundy.

1469 Birth of politician Machiavelli.
Lorenzo de' Medici rules Florence.
Death of Fra Filippo Lippi.

1471 Birth of Dürer.
Election of Pope Sixtus IV.

1472 Birth of Cranach the Elder.

1475 Birth of Michelangelo.
Death of Uccello.
Death of Dieric Bouts.

1476/78 Birth of Giorgione.

c.1478 Birth of Gossaert.
Giuliano de' Medici murdered during Pazzi conspiracy.

c.1480 Birth of Altdorfer.
Piero della Francesca writing mathematical treatises (1480s).

c.1481 Pacher completes *St. Wolfgang Altarpiece*.

1482 Death of Hugo van der Goes.
Death of Luca della Robbia.
Sixtus IV summons artists to Rome (including Botticelli, Perugino, and Ghirlandaio) to decorate Sistine Chapel.

1483 Van der Goes's *Portinari Altarpiece* arrives in Florence.
Birth of Martin Luther.
Birth of Raphael.
Charles VIII becomes King of France.
Richard III becomes King of England.

1485 Birth of Titian.
Alberti's *De Re Architectura* published.

Henry VII becomes King of England.

1486 Maximilian I elected King of Germany.

1488 Death of Verrocchio.

1489 Venice acquires Cyprus.

1492 Death of Piero della Francesca.
Innocent VIII elected Pope.
Columbus discovers West Indies.

1494 Political Wars in Italy.
Medici exiled from Florence.
Death of Ghirlandaio.
Birth of Pontormo.
Dürer makes first trip to Italy.

1495 Death of Cosimo Tura.
Birth of Jan van Scorel.

1497/98 Birth of Hans Holbein the Younger.

1498 Death of Antonio del Pollaiuolo.

c.1500–5 Bosch paints *St. Anthony Triptych*.

1501 Leonardo's famous cartoon (now lost) exhibited in Florence.
Michelangelo begins *David*.

1502 Leonardo appointed as Cesare Borgia's chief architect and military engineer.
Bramante completes *Tempietto*.

1503 Election of Pope Julius II.
Birth of Bronzino.
Birth of Parmigianino.

1505 Dürer makes second journey to Italy (returns 1507).
Giorgione paints "landscape", *Tempesta*.

1506 Discovery of the *Laocoön*.
Death of Mantegna.
Foundation stone laid for new St. Peter's.

1508 Michelangelo begins work on the Vatican Sistine Ceiling.

1509 Raphael begins work on the Vatican *stanze*.
Henry VIII becomes King of England.

1510 Death of Giorgione.

1511 Birth of Vasari.

1512 Sistine Ceiling unveiled.
Fall of Florentine Republic.

1513 Death of Pope Julius II.
Leo X elected Pope.
Medici restored in Florence.

1514 Death of Bramante.

1515 Grünewald completes *Isenheim Altarpiece*.
Doge's Palace completed in Venice.

Francis I becomes King of France

1516 Death of Bosch.
Death of Giovanni Bellini.

1517 Beginning of Reformation in Germany.

1518 Birth of Tintoretto.

1519 Death of Leonardo.
Charles V (King of Spain) becomes Holy Roman Emperor.

1520 Death of Raphael.

1521 Diet of Worms: Luther condemned by Church.
Death of Dürer.

1523 Death of Perugino.

1524 Death of Joachim Patenier.

1527 Sack of Rome by French imperial forces.
Death of Machiavelli.

1528 Publication of Castiglione's *Book of the Courtier*.
Birth of Veronese.
Death of Grünewald.
Publication of Dürer's treatise *On Human Proportion*.

1529 Sansovino made architect to the Venetian Republic.

1530 Correggio completes dome paintings in Parma Cathedral.
Death of Quinten Massys.

1532 Death of Gossaert.

1533 Holbein paints *The Ambassadors*.

1534 Luther's Bible published.
Henry VIII becomes head of Church of England, breaking with Rome.

1538 Publication of Holbein's *Dance of Death*.
Death of Altdorfer.

1540 Death of Parmigianino.

1543 Death of Holbein.

1545 Counter-Reformation begins.

1546 Death of Martin Luther.

1550 Publication of first edition of Vasari's *Lives of the Most Excellent Painters, Sculptors, and Architects*.

1553 Death of Cranach.

1556 Death of Pontormo.

1558 Elizabeth I becomes Queen of England.

1562 Death of Van Scorel.

1564 Death of Michelangelo.

1572 Death of Bronzino.

1576 Death of Titian.

1588 Death of Veronese.

1594 Death of Tintoretto.

View of Florence in the 15th century